INTRODUCING

MEDIA

PRACTICE

THE ESSENTIAL GUIDE

MATTHEW KERRY AND GEORGIA STONE

Los Angeles | London | New Delhi
Singapore | Washington DC | Melbourne

302.
23
KER

Los Angeles | London | New Delhi
Singapore | Washington DC | Melbourne

SAGE Publications Ltd
1 Oliver's Yard
55 City Road
London EC1Y 1SP

SAGE Publications Inc.
2455 Teller Road
Thousand Oaks, California 91320

SAGE Publications India Pvt Ltd
B 1/I 1 Mohan Cooperative Industrial Area
Mathura Road
New Delhi 110 044

SAGE Publications Asia-Pacific Pte Ltd
3 Church Street
#10-04 Samsung Hub
Singapore 049483

Editor: Michael Ainsley
Editorial assistant: John Nightingale
Production editor: Imogen Roome
Copyeditor: Neil Dowden
Proofreader: Clare Weaver
Indexer: Martin Hargreaves
Marketing manager: Lucia Sweet
Cover design: Jennifer Crisp
Typeset by: C&M Digitals (P) Ltd, Chennai, India
Printed in the UK

Icons from Noun Project: Chapter 1, 10 and 12 created by
Ralf Schmitzer. Chapter 2 created by corpus delicti. Chapter 3
created by Ramesha. Chapter 4 created by mikicon. Chapter 5
created by Creative Stall. Chapter 6 created by Viktor Ostrovsky.
Chapter 7 created by Thengakola. Chapter 8 created by Prasad.
Chapter 9 created by Creative Stall. Chapter 11 created by
Yu luck.

Library of Congress Control Number: 2017947189

British Library Cataloguing in Publication data

A catalogue record for this book is available from
the British Library

ISBN 978-1-4739-0652-5
ISBN 978-1-4739-0651-8 (pbk)

At SAGE we take sustainability seriously. Most of our products are printed in the UK using FSC papers and boards.
When we print overseas we ensure sustainable papers are used as measured by the PREPS grading system.
We undertake an annual audit to monitor our sustainability.

CONTENTS

PREFACE

How to Use This Book

This book serves as the core text for your undergraduate media course – especially where you are required to make links between practice and theory.

It aims to bring together the analytical and practical elements of media studies. Throughout the book there are topics (such as audience research and mise en scène) that will perhaps be familiar to you from theoretical modules and lectures. Or, there may be topics (such as writing and camerawork) that are first introduced to you during a practical project. These topics are clearly signposted throughout the book, so that you will be able to cross-reference between theory and practice during your course.

The topics will also be contextualised with an employability focus: enabling you to understand the real purpose of supporting practice with theory and vice versa. The main idea behind this book is that if you make stronger links between media practice and media theory, it will ultimately enhance your employability.

The exercises in the book can form the basis of a record of achievement and may be added to an ongoing portfolio. Alternatively, they may simply be exercises that you can initiate yourself to prepare you for a major project. The practical exercises in this book can be used to support your assessed project work and career planning and development.

We want to encourage you to have fun with this book! The more you practise through independent learning, the more you will enhance your professional development, and this may ultimately lead you to a successful career in the media and creative industries.

ACKNOWLEDGEMENTS

Michael Ainsley, John Nightingale, Delayna Spencer, Mila Steele and all at Sage who have helped us with the process of completing this book.

Tilly Stone, Shannon Holleworth, Martha Baker and Nazanin Ashkboos for their willingness to take part in the photo shoot.

Steve Lippert for his help with the graphics.

INTRODUCTION
Media Practice, Media Theory and Employability

Overview

This book will help you to consider media practice as a form of continuous career development, and to understand how practical media projects can enhance your employability. As a media student, you will most probably be on a course that has some combination of theory and practice. For example, you may be studying a media course that is mostly analytical, but has a small element of media practice. Or, on the other hand, you may be on a practice-based course that has some modules or lectures that focus on critical analysis that helps to contextualise your practical projects.

During your course you may find that you have a preference for theory over practice, or vice versa, and you may not always think about making a link between the two. However, by reading this book and carrying out some of the recommended exercises, you will find that an understanding of the purpose of your practical work can be improved by referring to theory and, conversely, your understanding of critical analysis can be enhanced, by putting it into practice! This all-encompassing approach to media studies will ultimately enhance your employability because an understanding of cultural contexts, audiences, meanings and effects will make you more desirable to future employers, over a prospective employee who only has technical skills.

If you are able to make strong links between media theory and practice, or can make a link between your practical work and employability in a broad careers sector, you will ultimately produce more satisfying work.

Media Theory and Media Practice

Professor Guy Starkey makes a convincing argument for using media practice as part of a theory-based media degree. He says that 'in the analysis of media texts, reception alone can be an insufficient approach', and that 'active learning' can be 'achieved by encoding *as well as* decoding' (Starkey, 2000). In other words, *producing* media texts can enable students to understand how meaning is constructed at the production stage of the communication process, as well as at the reception stage.

One of the classic misconceptions about the type of media course that you are on is that it is purely vocational, and that technology and technical skills are prioritised over content and purpose. This is not the case! Technical training is obviously beneficial to you, but only forms a minor part of your skills development. Let us put this into context. On non-practical modules you are not 'trained to read' or 'trained to write an essay' but this is something you learn to do through practice. Your lectures and seminars on theoretical modules discuss the content of your assignments: the topics, arguments and debates that you subsequently write about in your essays. It is through the practice of writing that your essay skills develop and improve.

Mike Wayne's ground-breaking book *Theorising Video Practice* (1997) was one of the first texts that asked media practitioners – like yourself – to consider their own work analytically. Wayne argues that we should read instruction manuals critically, and questions the inappropriate use of the terms 'natural' and 'naturalness' as an explanation of the way an image is read and understood by its audience (Wayne, 1997: 49). As you will see after reading this book, the production and content of media texts is anything but natural! Their 'naturalness' is the result of an ideological process, including choice of character, narrative construction, camera framing, editing and so on. You should think carefully about all of these elements when working on your own projects, and consider their effects on the audience.

The *Why* Not the *How*

On occasions, some instructional manuals do introduce elements of theory, and this can make a refreshing change because it helps the reader to actively think about the effects of their projects, rather than simply receiving technical instruction. In *Directing: Film Techniques and Aesthetics*, for example, Michael Rabiger says that white, male dominance in the media industries should be challenged, and asserts that entertainment *constructs* society, rather than *reflects* it (Rabiger, 2003: 8).

Kochberg's edited collection of essays on documentary production by the lecturing staff of the University of Portsmouth makes appropriate use of media theory. Marie Womack's chapter, for instance, considers how 'cultural reception of the same documentary varies according to the particular cultural context' (Kochberg, 2007: 59). She identifies that the 'production of meanings' in a documentary is not only prescribed by 'the documentary itself and its producer' but also by viewers, 'since people will get different meanings from the same documentary' (Kochberg, 2007: 61). To illustrate this point about contextualising the audience's experience she makes reference to Bourdieu's theory of 'cultural capital' – something you may be familiar with from your theoretical modules. She also highlights the importance of media theory as a strong element of audience research in pre-production planning (Kochberg, 2007: 73).

Our book includes some elements of instruction – it would not be a textbook if instructions were not included – but we are primarily interested in getting you to think about the 'why' rather than the 'how to' aspects of your projects. For example, we want you to ask yourself why a character should wear a particular costume, what the effect is of a particular setting on the rest of the story, and what significance age and gender has when used in a voice-over.

If you have previously been resistant to theory, we hope that by applying it to your own practical work, you will experience a series of 'eureka' moments, and see the connections between practice and theory on your course! This will help you to enjoy developing skills and confidence in media analysis and ultimately make you a more successful media student.

Media Practice and Employability

Rather than seeing media practice as a vocational route into the media industry, we prefer to argue that many of the skills that are acquired through media studies and media practice can be transferred to a great variety of employment contexts. For those who do want to enter the industry, however, Guy Starkey argues that employers 'want degree-calibre people with some relevant skills and experience who can quickly be brought up to speed *in situ*' adding 'a theoretical underpinning of practical applications is a bonus, and later in their careers it might differentiate the media graduates who have encountered semiotics from those with other specialisms who have not' (Starkey, 2000).

Acquiring an appreciation of the role of analysis in your media practice can also enhance your employability. It will enable you to critically analyse and reflect on your own working practices and your own media texts. Having skills in critical analysis will be seen as a bonus in the eyes of your future employers.

A focus on teamwork and team dynamics will also be explored throughout the book. Practical production work by its very nature relies on teamwork and communication skills. Many of the exercises aim to boost your confidence and abilities in public speaking, and subsequently prepare you for the world of work.

The Structure of the Book

The book is structured in a logical progression from establishing teams to the exhibition of your work, and finally to becoming career ready. However, it need not necessarily be followed in this order from cover to cover. It is written in a way that enables you to select reading and exercises that will be useful at particular times during your course, for a number of different projects.

A series of suggested classroom or workshop exercises appear throughout the book, and independent learning tasks such as an indication of further reading, research or building a portfolio are introduced at various times to assist your practical work. The book also gives guidance on how to work with external clients as part of project-based work experience.

The structure of the chapters is as follows:

> Chapter 1 **Media Practice and Employability** explains that media-practice projects can be considered as ongoing work experience. It discusses the relationship between the projects and transferable skills. The practical exercises will give you a sense of where and how you might use the experience of media practice on your degree course in your future career development.

Chapter 2 **Media Production Teams** will enable you to identify the importance of team dynamics and to make a strong link between teamwork and employability. A series of exercises will be introduced to help you construct teams and to assign team roles effectively.

Before you embark on your projects it may be useful to consider your work in an industrial context. Chapter 3 **Media Project Briefs** looks at the importance of working to a brief, liaising with a brief provider, and also how you can work up your own brief for a specific market. Transferable skills in communication, project management and organisation are emphasised here. Importantly, the chapter highlights the benefits of applying skills acquired through media practice to a wide variety of employment contexts.

Chapter 4 focuses on the topic of **Audiences**. It looks at theoretical approaches to audience research in order to understand how real audiences use media texts as part of their daily lives. You will be encouraged and assisted in carrying out audience research as part of your pre-production planning.

Chapter 5 **Scripting Your Projects** looks at different aspects of writing for media. It is informed by theories regarding media forms, genres and narrative construction. The chapter includes guided exercises to support scripting, storyboarding and pitching ideas. The latter is a skill that can boost confidence and ultimately be applied to variety of careers.

An analysis of the design elements of audio visual communication appears in Chapter 6 on **Designing Your Projects**. This chapter will enable you to consider how you should use these theoretical tools to inform the production of your own work. For example, when designing 'people' for a media-practice project, class, gender, sexuality and ethnicity should be considered.

Chapter 7 **Constructing Your Projects** examines the use of lighting, use of colour and the framing of images. Importantly, it asks you to think about the meanings and effects that are constructed by the technical elements of media practice.

Chapter 8 covers the **Media Production** of your projects. It includes information on production roles and production duties, and discusses administration documents that will help you to organise your work.

Editing Your Projects is the subject of Chapter 9. An analysis of image and sound editing, and the use of typography in your projects is included here.

Chapter 10 **Exhibition and Distribution** will enable you to pilot and disseminate your work. The chapter includes information on preparing your projects for online distribution, festivals and guidance on arranging your own screening.

Chapter 11 is an investigation into **Critical Analysis and Reflection**. It will enable you to analyse your own productions using media theory, and to critically reflect on your working practices. This chapter is particularly useful for when you write reflective essays about your own work.

Finally, in Chapter 12 **Employability and Media Practice** we will summarise how to use the skills and experience from previous chapters, and consider how this can feed into potential future careers. You will be encouraged to identify transferable skills from your projects and consider how these can be used in career development and planning.

This introduction has revealed the contents, aims and structure of the book, and has suggested how the different elements of your course relate to each other. In particular it has emphasised the relevance of media theory to your practical work, and explained how you should make connections between theoretical approaches and real life skills.

Now – let's get started!

FIGURE 0.1
Media production team

1

MEDIA PRACTICE AND
EMPLOYABILITY
From Project Skills to Real-World Skills

After reading this chapter you will be able to:

- understand the relationship between your media degree, media-practice projects and transferable employability skills;
- understand the value of media-practice project work to your future employability;
- understand how you might design your career path whilst engaged with media-practice project work;
- examine potential career routes and destinations from your media degree course.

Introduction

This chapter concerns itself with the link between media practice and employability, considering how a range of important skills appropriate to the jobs market can be developed through engaging with media-practice work on your degree course. Media-practice projects can be considered as ongoing work experience. They are more than just making media texts or products for coursework and developing practical or technical skills.

In a sense, we are starting at the end with an exploration of your potential career route upon graduation. This chapter aims to help broaden your horizons and focus on the skillsets you may need for a variety of different routes from your media degree. It will focus on a wide range of transferable skills into a number of career areas in the media, creative and communications industries.

Career/Personal Development Portfolios

It is valuable to keep a record of your media-practice work throughout your degree course in the form of a portfolio. This will help to keep your ideas in one place, it will be useful for your career planning and it may be useful for assessment purposes. You can also refer to it to inform any critical analysis and reflection that may be required of you on your course.

Such a portfolio is essentially a reflective journal. A reflective journal can take any form – written, video or in an audio form. Potential employers recommend keeping a journal or portfolio. A report prepared by the CBI (Confederation of British Industry) and the NUS (National Union of Students) entitled *Working Towards Your Future: Making the Most of Your Time in HE* (2011) recommends keeping a record of your developing employability skills as you go along. Such a portfolio, some-times labelled a personal development portfolio (PDP), will ideally reflect your experience and also give evidence of your learning. The CBI/NUS suggest that 'there's a big difference between asserting that you can learn and change and being able to point to concrete evidence of having done so'. They recommend you could do this through answering the following questions.

- What went wrong with something you were organising or doing?
- What did you learn from this situation?
- What did you do different the next time round to avoid the same problem arising? (CBI/NUS, 2011: 36)

EXERCISE
Career/Personal Development Portfolio

This is a good point at which to start a portfolio for yourself. Decide what format you will use for it. A range of apps are available online for building a portfolio. Alternatively, you could produce it in an audio or audio visual form. So, make a start with your portfolio and resolve to keep it updated from now on! You can pick and choose from the exercises in this book to add to it. Hopefully, you will end with a useful tool to assist you in entering your career when you graduate.

Career Routes and Destinations

Let's start by looking ahead to graduating from your degree and thinking about what your career destination might be. Imagine it is the day after the graduation ceremony and the subsequent celebrations. You are no longer a student, you have your whole future ahead of you, and now it is time to enter the 'real' world of work! What plans have you got in place? How will you use your degree to enter that rather scary world?

A good starting point is to clarify what characterises the career area into which you might enter on graduation. To consider what transferable skills and knowledge you have developed through your degree as a whole, and through media-practice work in particular that will be useful to the workplace.

Suitable Careers with a Media Degree?

If you use the keyword 'media' when searching online for jobs, you will be presented with quite a narrow range of careers, such as in media sales. Try broadening your search terms by looking at the creative industries. By looking at the creative industries as a potential employment field, rather than the narrow field of media careers, you are already broadening your horizons into a wide field of employment areas appropriate to your degree qualification, skills and experience. There are at least three sectors that may be appropriate areas to start your careers search from your media studies degree. These sectors are defined by Prospects.ac.uk as: 'Creative Arts and Culture', 'Media and Publishing' and 'Marketing, Advertising and Public Relations'.

What Are the Creative Industries?

The creative industries are wide-ranging and fast-moving sectors. A search will reveal the following list of just a few of the potential careers that might be suitable for you on graduation, armed with your media degree:

public relations officer	film runner	magazine journalist
animator	advertising account executive	communications consultant
radio producer	computer games publisher	video runner
press agent	books publisher	media planner
marketing executive	scriptwriter	creative director
video editor	information officer	magazine publisher
media producer	researcher	broadcast journalist

FIGURE 1.1
Potential careers for media degree graduates

And many more!

So, the creative industry sector is a broad field for potential employment and an appropriate route from a media degree. It is also important to many other employment sectors. For example, marketing and public relations departments exist in most non-media organisations, both large and small, corporate and third sector, so you may end up working in an organisation that has little connection with the media itself, but within the media side of that organisation.

EXERCISE
Highlighting Potential Jobs/Employment Areas

Look at the list of possible jobs to come out of a media degree in Figure 1.1 above and highlight one of the potential jobs that might be of interest to you, or one that you know little about at the moment. Investigate the following aspects of the role:

- The job description.
- The person specification.
- The location.
- Where the jobs are advertised.
- A live example of a job advertisement.
- The trade press associated with the job.
- The promotion and career structure.
- The salary levels.

Follow this up by finding a case study of someone currently working in the job in focus. Careers case studies can be found on a number of websites online. Start by looking at the websites suggested in the further reading section at the end of this chapter.

Using your research as a basis, create a handout, a presentation, a web page or an infographic poster aimed at your peers on your degree course. Your aim should be to give them all the information they need about the job you chose to focus on. You could add this to your career/personal development portfolio to give you a starting point in your career planning. Repeat this exercise for any other jobs that you think might appeal to you.

What Is It Like to Work in the Creative Industries?

In our experience, graduates go into the creative industries sector due to a passion for the work and lifestyle rather than for just the money. Often, they could earn more in a different area of employment, or have much better job security but they are attracted to working in the creative sector.

In order to start to think about what sort of career would suit you, the following exercise will help you to examine your general aspirations in career terms.

EXERCISE
Career Pros and Cons

When thinking of which employment area might suit you best, it is worth thinking about what constitutes 'good work' for you. This will be a very individual thing. To explore this, pick out five features from the table in Figure 1.2 that define what constitutes 'good work' for you personally. Put these in rank order from 1 to 5 and give a brief explanation of why you have chosen each. This should help you to start to focus on your general needs career wise, rather than being too specific about particular jobs at this stage in your career planning.

Lots of variety	Control over own workload	Lots of interest
Lots of salary potential	Amount of responsibility	Possibility for flexible working
Possibility for teamwork	Potential for involvement in decision making	Lots of independence
Training opportunities	Travel opportunities	Opportunities for professional development
Opportunities for career progression and promotion	Good job security	Good work colleagues
Ability to control work–life balance	Ability to develop leadership and management skills	Social aspects of the job

FIGURE 1.2
Career pros and cons

Now, think about how the characteristics of work in the creative industries below chime with your own evaluation of what constitutes a 'good job' for you.

- Very creative
- Driven by deadlines
- Driven by targets
- Often includes travel opportunities
- Often involves long hours
- Sometimes involves unsociable hours
- Often freelance and self-employed
- Sometimes part-time work and a portfolio career
- Level of income unpredictable
- Involves lots of teamwork
- Involves a lot of autonomy and need for being proactive

Are you still convinced?

Next, look at each of the characteristics of work in the creative industries above and identify some evidence from your experience so far that suggests that you should pursue this career area further. You could give examples of when you have had to work long and flexible hours, for example, and evaluate how this suits your personality type and your career aspirations.

Add the results of this exercise to your portfolio for future reference. This will help you when thinking about what characterises the sort of work you would like (and not like!) to experience in future.

Degrees, Media Studies and Employability

Having identified some of the key features of the work sector you might enter on graduation, we now turn our attention to thinking about how your university experience in general and your media studies degree in particular will help prepare you for employment in the media and creative industries sector.

Many careers and employability advisory services suggest that almost any degree you do will prepare you for a career in media. Clearly though, a degree in a media-related area will put you at an advantage. On your media-based degree course, you are focusing on the development of the following generic skills, which amongst others will be useful for a future career in the media, communications and creative industry.

Critical analysis skills

Research skills

Commercial awareness

Cultural awareness

Teamwork skills

Creative skills

Writing skills

Flexibility

Working to briefs

Time management

Communication skills

Critical reflection skills

Problem solving

People skills

Reflect on some of the above and think about how your course to date has helped you to develop and improve these skills. Think also about specific examples and contexts where you have applied them, such as through project work, essay work, through media project or essay work.

Learning from Alumni about Potential Career Routes

Alumni are graduates or former students from your degree course. All universities have a department dedicated to keeping in touch with their alumni. You can learn a lot from finding out where graduates from your degree have gone onto after graduating and you can learn a lot from your degree course's alumni. The following exercises will help you to do this.

EXERCISE
Destinations

This exercise will help you to explore the career destinations of previous students from your degree course. Take a look at the destinations statistics and information about where media graduates go after their degree. In the UK, you can find this information on the HECSU (Higher Education Careers Services Unit) website at www.hecsu.ac.uk. Here you can download the latest report entitled 'What Do Graduates Do Survey'. This is a survey of UK graduates undertaken annually six months after graduating which analyses where students from different degree courses are working at that point in time. There are clearly problems with the fact that the survey is based on careers only six months after graduation, but it does give a sense of where graduates go after their degree. Have a look at the findings for your own degree area.

Using this information as a basis, create a handout, presentation or infographic poster about the career destinations of students from your own degree course. Aim this at your peers or at prospective students of your degree. Think about what you have learned from this research that impacts on your decision-making process for your career plan. You could add the results of this exercise to your career development portfolio for future reference.

EXERCISE
Alumni Web Pages

Another way to learn from the alumni of your university is to look at your university's alumni web pages. For this exercise, pick out one case study of interest to you and your degree or future career aspiration. Share the chosen profile with your peers, explaining how the person has progressed in their career since graduation. You might consider the following questions:

- What degree course did they do?
- What career are they in now, and how did they reach that career?
- How did they use their degree in order to enter the career area?

EXERCISE
Interviewing Alumni

Alumni from your degree course are a rich resource of knowledge and advice for you and it is a good idea to reflect on their experience and knowledge to inform your own decisions about your career path. A valuable exercise is to question alumni from your degree course about how they have achieved what they have and where their degree has taken them, how and why.

For this exercise, think about the questions you would ask of alumni of your degree course about your potential career route. Think about what you would like to know or learn from them about their career since graduating. Choose six of the questions from the table in Figure 1.3 and arrange an interview with an alumnus of your course or with someone who is in the career area you aspire to. Once you have conducted the interview you could produce a case-study video or audio piece, write it up as an article for your student-union newspaper or prepare a presentation for your peers. This would be a useful exercise to add to your developing career/personal development portfolio.

When did you graduate and what was your degree title?
Can you give a timeline of your career since graduating?
How do you achieve an acceptable work–life balance?
Was your first job advertised? If so, where was it advertised and how did you find it?
How important was your degree result to your career so far?
How much networking do you do in your daily job and how important is it?
How important is the use of social media in your work? Which do you use and which do you not use and why?
Which three skills you learned through your degree course do you use in your job?
What is the difference between being a student and being a professional?
Does your job involve teamwork?
What is a typical working day or week for you?
What professional development and training do you have in your job?
What are the career progression routes in your job?
Do you see your job as having social aspects?
Do you have to observe a dress code in your job?
What is your workplace environment like?
What is the most important skill in your job?
What one piece of advice would you give to students who aspire to a career in the media, communications and creative industries sector?

FIGURE 1.3
Questions for interviewing alumni of media degrees

EXERCISE
Job Advert for Your Ideal Job

The following exercise will help you to focus on specific jobs that you might be interested in and to find out the detailed requirements of them. Use what you have learned so far about your ideal career to produce an advert for the job you would like on graduation. Most job adverts include the following information:

- The job title.
- The location of the job (be specific about city and country).
- Details of the salary range.
- The name of the company.
- A job description including a list of roles and responsibilities.
- A person specification describing the 'ideal' candidate.
- A list of skills and experience in a bulleted list identifying those that are essential and those that are desirable for the role.
- Details of the organisation with information about the sector and its position within it.
- Information about the organisation's culture and aspirations.
- Instructions about how to apply for the job (CV and cover email/letter, application form, etc.).

Use this to construct your ideal job description. Once you have produced this, you could follow it up by preparing a presentation for your peers about the job you have researched. Your presentation should aim to give them a detailed insight into the job you are focusing on. This would be a good piece of research to add to your personal/career development portfolio.

Examining Employers' Expectations

So far, we have looked at the career sector you might aspire to enter on graduating from your media studies degree. We have looked at the sorts of jobs that exist in the media, communications and creative industries and how you might start to work towards them whilst on your degree course. Let's now think about matching the skills that employers are looking for with the skills you are likely to develop on your degree course generally, and also specifically through any media-practice project work you may be engaged with.

Most employers are less interested in the degree subject you studied than the wider range of skills, qualities and experience you can demonstrate. Employers generally value the skills associated with the student's degree such as the intellectual and practical skills, but importantly a variety of 'soft skills'.

According to Cottrell (2008: 35) these are very general personal skills that include such areas as:

- self-awareness;
- self-reflection;
- showing initiative;
- motivation.

Interpersonal skills are also seen as important, for example having:

- teamworking skills;
- leadership and management skills;
- communication skills;
- cultural awareness.

Finally, skills around managing projects are important, such as:

- problem-solving and project-management skills;
- being flexible;
- ability to work to a brief.

A report produced by the CBI (Confederation for British Industry) titled *Future Fit: Preparing Graduates for the World of Work* (2009) suggests that: 'Underpinning all these attributes, the key foundation, must be a positive attitude: a "can-do" approach, a readiness to take part and contribute, openness to new ideas and a drive to make these happen' (CBI and Universities UK, 2009: 8).

In addition to this, having a wider cultural awareness relating to the workplace links directly to your experiences as a student on a media degree. By working on both analytical and practical modules, you will be able to make links between practice and theory, and this will provide you with the 'cultural references' and 'vocabulary' that creative industries employers find attractive in an employee.

It is clearly important to have a range of skills for work in the creative industries sector including 'soft skills' as well as 'hard skills'. 'Soft skills' are transferable between many different jobs and include general communication skills, project-management and people skills as detailed above. 'Hard skills', on the other hand, are directly related to a specific job, for example the use of specialist software and technical camera skills. So clearly, the soft skills involved in your media projects, such as 'communication', 'problem-solving' and 'people skills' are just as important, if not more so, than 'hard skills' such as ability to operate a camcorder or to edit using a specific program. Additionally, 'soft skills' can potentially be transferred to any number of jobs when compared to 'hard skills'.

The table in Figure 1.4 lists examples of person specifications for work in the media and creative industry sector. They have been synthesised from a large number of person specifications for a range of jobs in the creative industries. You can see how important the 'soft skills' described above are to employers.

Has proven exceptional communication skills, both written and verbal.	Is capable of managing own workload in order to meet conflicting deadlines.	Has ability to remain focused and see a project through to completion to a high standard.	Is customer and market focused.
Shows evidence of good planning and time management, self-organisation and self-discipline.	Shows initiative and is proactive and able to work independently.	Is able to work with others and in a team effectively.	Is dependable and takes responsibility for own actions and keeps commitments.
Has research ability and analytical skill.	Is innovative and creative; good at problem-solving.	Has interpersonal and relationship management skills.	Understands direct marketing principles, processes and channels.
Understands copywriting fundamentals.	Understands the application of technology to secure the best marketing outcomes.	Has budgeting knowledge and experience.	Understands the principles of negotiation.
Has excellent writing and communication skills.	Has an enthusiastic and outgoing attitude.	Has fantastic organisation skills.	Holds a clean driving licence.
Has excellent and proven administrative skills.	Shows excellent communication, presentation and interpersonal skills.	Is well organised and flexible in their approach to their work.	Is able to work to given deadlines and cope with periodic sudden increases in workload.
Is a clear team player.	Can demonstrate good customer-service skills.	Is technology-friendly and has familiarity with operating a range of audio-visual equipment.	Has a genuine knowledge and interest in film and television industries.
Has demonstrable research skills.	Has good knowledge of web technologies, content management systems and digital communication platforms and awareness of web trends.	Has excellent written and verbal communication skills.	Demonstrates excellent interpersonal skills and the ability to build positive working relationships.
Has clear experience of managing social media channels in a professional setting.	Is prepared to work for gaining the experience needed.	Is highly motivated and goal orientated.	Is enthusiastic, outgoing and resilient.

(Continued)

Is polite and tactful with the ability to act with discretion and sensitivity in dealing with confidential matters.	Has the ability to prioritise, multi-task and work under pressure.	Shows the ability to work successfully both within a team and on one's own initiative.	Shows a willingness to work occasional evenings and weekends and unsocial hours.

FIGURE 1.4
Person specifications for jobs in the media and creative industries

How many of the 'soft skills' areas can you find evidence of having at this stage in your degree?

Let's move on to considering the sorts of skills you might start to focus on now.

EXERCISE
Mock Jobs Search Exploring Person Specifications and Key Skills

This exercise aims to get you thinking about the specific skills (including hard and soft skills) required for the jobs that interest you. Most job advertisements include a job description, followed by a list of responsibilities that come with the job and a person specification or list of requirements of the applicant. This will be a list of the skills and knowledge that are essential to the job.

For this exercise, look at websites where there are graduate jobs advertised in the sector you are interested in. There are some suggestions of places you might look at the end of this chapter. Bookmark around four of the jobs on offer that appeal to you and look at the **person specifications** for each of your chosen jobs. Create a list of the **person specs** and/or **requirements** for all of the four chosen jobs by cutting and pasting from the adverts. Next, paste *all* the lists of person specs and job requirements from the four jobs you are looking at into a word cloud app. This should help you to identify the most common skills, knowledge and qualities required for the jobs you are focusing on as in the example in Figure 1.5 below. The four jobs in this example were graduate-level digital marketing and communications jobs.

Identify the most commonly occurring words (i.e. those that are largest) in the word cloud you have created.

- What sort of skills, knowledge and experience are employers looking for?
- What do you need to do for you to be ready to apply for such jobs?

You could follow this up by producing a handout, an infographic poster or a presentation about your findings to share with your peers. Adding the results of this exercise to your personal development portfolio will help you to see your career development more clearly.

FIGURE 1.5
Word cloud for person specifications required for graduate marketing and communications jobs

Summary

We have seen in this chapter that thinking now about the sector in which you might ultimately end up working and the *general skills* you can build throughout your media degree can be very useful to you. Being engaged with practical media project work whilst on your degree is a useful place to start building the required skills, experience, knowledge and networks to find employment in the media and creative industries sector.

It is not just the practical skills you will gain and develop through media practice that makes media project work important to your future career, but an awareness that the organisational structures of the creative industries are similar to those of your media project work. Any media-practice project work you do at university is an important simulation of the sector you may graduate into. You will gain valuable employability skills through media-practice work on your degree. These skills areas will be visited throughout this book as you develop your media-practice project work.

In Chapter 2 we will move on to consider the personal and teamwork skills required for successful projects. We will be reflecting on the idea that employers require evidence of deep understanding and proven skills in many areas, which you will need to demonstrate.

Further Reading

The following websites will be useful to you in your careers research in addition to any you find yourself. Your employability department should be able to point you to specific sites for job adverts for your particular career area.

> **Creative Choices** – ccskills.org.uk – this website is aimed at young people who are taking their first steps in careers in the creative sector. It includes careers advice, job adverts and profiles of a range of jobs in the sector.
>
> **Creative Skillset** – creativeskillset.org – this website has a good A to Z of job roles in the creative industries as well as listing job vacancies.
>
> **Guardian Careers** – theguardian.com/careers – this website has some focused advice around general careers as well as some case studies and profiles of jobs in many sectors of the media industries.
>
> **Mediargh** – www.mediargh.com – this website has some careers advice but is more focused on advertising media jobs and internships. Very popular with students.
>
> **Prospects** – www.prospects.ac.uk – this website is very often used in higher education for developing employability. It has useful careers advice pages and some very useful case studies and profiles of jobs in different sectors. It also includes adverts for jobs, internships and work experience.
>
> **Shooting People** – shootingpeople.org – this is a website focused on the independent film sector with job adverts and opportunities to connect with a community of film-makers.
>
> **The Unit List** – www.theunitlist.com – this website focuses on jobs in TV with some advice aimed specifically at television careers.

Cottrell, Stella, 2008, *The Study Skills Handbook*, London: Palgrave Macmillan.
An excellent core textbook for supporting your higher education experience with some useful exercises around employability.

Davies, Rosamund and Sigthorsson, Gauti, 2013, *Introducing the Creative Industries from Theory to Practice*, London: Sage.
An essential guide to the make-up of the creative industries with some useful case studies and interviews with people in the industry about their career.

2

MEDIA PRODUCTION TEAMS
Team Skills and Life Skills

After reading this chapter you will be able to:

- understand the importance of working as part of a team in any media-practice project work;
- understand team dynamics and their importance;
- understand the benefits of assigning roles to different members of a team at different points in any project;
- make a link between teamwork skills and your own developing employability.

Introduction

We have seen in the last chapter that careers in the media and creative industries require many skills that can be developed through media-practice project work. We will see in this chapter that the creative industries are dominated by freelancers. Networking is therefore essential for getting work. A proven ability to work within a team on a practical media project is an essential skill to show evidence of when applying for, or pitching for, jobs.

Teamwork in the Media and Creative Industries as an Employability Skill

Before you start to build the team for your media project, it is important to consider why teamwork is such an important skill. Students often complain of the need for so much group work on media courses, but experience in teamwork can be very beneficial in education.

A project titled Group Work and Assessment in Media Practice (GWAMP, 2003) identified some of the advantages of group work in media practice as follows:

- Group work enables higher-quality and larger-scale work than can be achieved through an individual project.

- Group work is more student-centred than teacher-directed thus helping students to be more autonomous.

- The pressure to contribute to the group's work can increase commitment which can, in turn, increase quality of the outcome of the project.

Most importantly, in the context of employment in the media and creative industries, teamwork is a key feature of almost any job role. You will quite often achieve more through teamwork compared to what can be achieved when working on your own. The skills you are required to use within team projects may be more diverse than if you were to work on your own. Teamwork also encourages the development of your interpersonal skills and it also promotes the development of leadership and management skills. All these are important to many areas of employment.

Any consideration of and planning for teamwork should begin with thinking about your own strengths and weaknesses. This will help you to consider how you can best contribute to effective media project collaboration and also what you might achieve from being engaged in teamwork. The following exercise will help you to identify your own strengths and what you have to offer, and also areas that you would benefit from developing.

EXERCISE
Personal Media Profiling

We suggest that you start by preparing a media profile to use when building a team for your project. This requires you to detail and reflect on your previous experience of collaborative project work. This exercise aims to support you in identifying relevant past experience and it will be useful in setting up a project team.

Prepare a 'media profile' by answering the questions below about your experience of working on a practical media project (or similar teamwork project) in the recent past:

- Media form – what media form did the project use?

- Purpose – what was the media project produced for? A course, a hobby, a competition?

- Your role – what roles did you take on during the life of the project?

- Skills demonstrated – what skills did you demonstrate through this project? Give a list of at least three.

- Skills to be improved – what skills would you like to have improved through the project? Give a list of at least three.

Use this information to write a short personal media profile. This written profile could be used as a basis to introduce yourself to others when it comes to building a media project team. You can add this to your career development portfolio and update it as new skills are acquired.

EXERCISE
Strengths and Weaknesses for Practical Media Project Work

This exercise will help you to interrogate your strengths and weaknesses further, specifically focusing on skills for practical media project work. Figure 2.1 shows a list of statements about how individuals might operate in a team. Select some statements from each list (strengths and weaknesses) that might have been said about you at some point during a group project in the past.

Strengths in relation to individual contribution to a group project

Shows enthusiasm for the project, and encourages enthusiasm in others.	Listens to and supports everyone's ideas.	Very good at completing tasks straight away. Stops the team from prevaricating.	Is able to solve problems by being flexible.
Has good creative vision and lots of ideas.	Pays good attention to detail, with keen awareness of quality control.	Has good technical ability.	Is very conscientious and hard working in all aspects of the project.
Sets goals, is highly motivated and holds the group together.	Good at networking and communication.	Has good attendance and engagement with the project.	Is a co-operative team member. Works well with others to a shared purpose.

Weaknesses in relation to individual contribution to a group project

Makes little contribution to the project, other than in what they feel comfortable with.	Does not take the initiative to complete a task without being asked.	Shies away from important decisions.	Attendance and engagement with the project wanes after the first few meetings.
Too concerned with the problems presented by the project than the reality of the situation.	Is over-confident and unable to take advice from others.	Sometimes prioritises other commitments such as work and other coursework deadlines.	Can be over-optimistic with what they can achieve. Overly critical of own and others' work.
Is only interesting in the technical side of the project.	Lacks attention to detail. Has a 'this'll do' attitude.	Can be quite bossy, and takes too much control over the project.	Does not work effectively as part of a group.

FIGURE 2.1
Strengths and weaknesses in relation to individual contribution to a group practical media project

Reflect on what your own strengths and weaknesses might be in working on a media project by giving an example or evidence to support each of the strengths and weaknesses you have picked out from the tables above.

You can now use this to formulate a personal 'action plan' for your approach to any practical media project you are engaged with by considering the following:

- List your current skills and qualities in working on a practical media project.
- Identify what you need to improve for successful project work.
- Develop a plan of action to improve your project skills – what you are going to do to improve and develop your skills.
- Identify how you will know that you have improved each of the areas you have identified.

Building Media-Practice Project Teams: Group-Project Dynamics and Individual Characteristics

It is important that you pay attention to the make-up of your team for any project you embark on. This can make or break the success of a project. From our experience of observing students working in project groups we have identified six typical characteristics of individual members. We have designed the following model to enable you to recognise yourself and the types of people you might work with on practical media projects. Our descriptions here are aimed at helping you to realise the potential problems that could occur during group work, and the exercises that follow will help you to avoid them. You are sure to recognise the descriptors below from your experience of teamwork and hopefully you will be able to identify yourself amongst the descriptors!

The group-project dynamics and individual characteristics we have identified are as follows:

The absentee: This person does not work effectively as part of a team. They are often absent and prefer to work on their own. They have poor communication skills, and lack commitment to a shared purpose. They will follow others' lead and contribute little of value or relevance to the project. Their organisational skills will be disruptive of the team. This student is likely to fail where individual contribution to a team project is assessed.

The clock-watcher: This group member's attendance and engagement with the project subsides after a positive and proactive start. They offer a reasonable amount to the project, but tend to stick within their comfort zone throughout. They lack attention to detail and have a 'this'll do' attitude to their work. This student will most probably end with a third-class grade for their individual contribution to the media project.

The good teamworker: This person has good attendance and engagement with the project. They follow rather than lead others, and might shy away from the important decisions. Or they might have unrealistic aims for the project. They sometimes prioritise other commitments such as their leisure pursuits, work and other coursework deadlines. Their communication and organisational skills could be improved. This student is likely to get a 2:2 grade for their individual contribution to the project.

The overseer: This group member is very conscientious, and extremely hard working in all aspects of the project. However, this might be to their downfall. They may be seen as being quite bossy, taking too much control over the project. Their leadership is not effective, in that it may fragment the group. This person can be overconfident and unable to take advice from others. Or they can be overly critical of their own and others' work. Although this student is very hard working, a grade of a 2:2 or low 2:1 for their individual contribution may reflect a weakness in team-working skills.

The very good teamworker: This group member is very co-operative within the group. They show initiative, they stop the team from prevaricating and are very good at completing tasks straight away. They can solve problems by being flexible. They have good creative vision and lots of ideas. They are very good at communicating and have well-developed networking skills. This student will probably be rewarded with a 2:1 grade for their individual work.

The first-class teamworker: This team member has excellent leadership qualities. They thrive on challenges and enjoy taking responsibility. They set goals, and are highly motivated. They hold the group together. They show lots of enthusiasm for the project, and encourage enthusiasm in others. They listen to and support everyone else's ideas. They have a keen awareness of quality control, and an excellent attention to detail. They work well with others to a shared purpose. This is an example of a student who will most probably receive a first-class mark for their individual contribution to the teamwork.

EXERCISE
Investigating Individual Teamwork Characteristics

Familiarise yourself with the features of the six descriptions we have outlined above. Decide which best matches you according to previous teamwork experience.

Consider how you would answer the question often asked in job interviews: 'How would fellow team members describe you?'

Draft a response, giving evidence and examples from previous projects to illustrate it. Add this to your portfolio of work. It could be useful for preparing for future job interviews, but also for preparing to be the best team member that you can be!

After investigating these team dynamics, you should consider what strategies you might use to avoid the negatives and enhance the positive aspects of group-project work in order to achieve success.

Forming Project Teams for Practical Media Project Work

Having put some thought into the team-related skills required for successful teamwork, you are now ready to start building the group for your media-practice project. One way you could do this is through some networking activities with your peers and potential team members. It is important that if your team is to be self-chosen, you do not take the seemingly easy option to work with friends. Moving out of your comfort zone and thinking about the roles, experience, strengths and weaknesses that you can contribute to a successful team will help in the long run. The following exercises will help you network with your peers in order to build an effective team for a media project.

EXERCISE
Plan an Elevator Pitch

Use what you have covered above about the ideal skills and competencies in relation to teamwork to prepare and perform an 'elevator pitch' about yourself. Being able to pitch is a skill that may be of value to you in future employment and at networking events. Networking is an important employability skill for work in many areas of the media and creative industries and being able to plan and deliver an effective pitch will be invaluable for this.

An elevator pitch is a way to sell yourself, an idea or a service. In this context it is intended as a way of selling yourself to potential team members for a media project. It is called an elevator pitch because it requires you to complete a presentation in the time it might take to get to the top floor of a tall building in an elevator. It has the following requirements:

- Your pitch should be 90 seconds in length. Plan your timings for it on the basis of three words per second. So, a 90-second pitch will be approximately 270 words long.

- Be clear about your goal for the pitch – what do you want to achieve from doing it? One of the main aims in this context should be for you to sell yourself to your peers as a potential team member for a media project.

- Complete the form below (Figure 2.2). In answering the questions, you should consider the areas we have discussed so far in this chapter about what would make you a good team member to choose. Think about the media profile produced through the exercise above. Think about your previous experience of teamwork around a media project. Think about what has been covered on transferable skills and also about what characterises your own approach to teamwork. In other words, think about what type of project team member you tend to be from the model above.

- Your pitch should be concise. It should help to solve a problem – in this case the problem of team membership. Why should you be chosen as a member of this team?

- Your pitch should avoid the use of technical or academic language and you should keep it simple, using plain English.

- You should be aware of your audience and address them effectively in a way that grabs their attention. Remember that your audience in this context is potential fellow team members.

- It is important to rehearse your pitch (perhaps in front of the mirror) checking for body language and fluency (in other words, do not read directly from crib sheets). You may choose to use props for your pitch to add to the information you are giving.

Use the form below to plan your pitch.

Media Project Team Pitch		
Aim for the pitch		
Objectives for the pitch (what you want to achieve)		
Timing/length of the pitch		
Props to be used in the pitch (if any)		
Content (not necessarily in the order below)	**Your notes**	**Timing (at rate of three words per second)**
Your name and main details.		
Welcome and introduction. Establish what you want to achieve through the pitch.		
Describe your area of expertise that is appropriate to the team being built.		
Talk about your past successes in similar project work.		
What makes you the best choice of team member – i.e. what is your unique selling point (USP)?		
Identify the 'value proposition' – i.e. what problem would be solved by your involvement in a project team.		
Define your 'pain statement' – i.e. why are you needed?		
Finish with a 'call to action' explaining what you want the audience to do as a result of hearing your pitch.		

FIGURE 2.2
Crib sheet for an elevator pitch

EXERCISE
Mini-Interview

Another way of networking with your peers to build a project team is to conduct a mini-interview with prospective team members. Below is a list of the sorts of questions used in so-called 'strengths-based' job interviews. Choose one question from the list below and make notes on how you would answer it in an interview situation.

- Tell me about an activity or task that comes easily to you.
- What activities give you an energy buzz?
- Tell me about something you are particularly proud of.
- Are you a starter or a finisher?
- What qualities would you bring to this team?
- Are you a big picture or a detail person?
- What do you find is always left until last/unfinished on your to-do-list?

(www.ed.ac.uk, accessed April 2015)

Include in your answer information about your typical characteristics as a team member, and past experience of teamwork. You could use the STAR mnemonic below to guide your answer to the chosen question as follows:

- **S**ituation – describe a situation you have experienced. In this context, it could be a recent teamwork-related experience you have had.
- **T**ask – describe what you were hoping to achieve from the situation you are focusing on.
- **A**ction – describe what you actually did in the situation.
- **R**esult – describe the outcome and what you achieved.

An additional **R** to the mnemonic above is useful to guide your *reflection* on the situation you are describing.

- **R**eflection – describe what you learned through the situation, whether and how you have experienced the same situation again, and how you might use this experience to inform future approaches to similar situations.

Once you have drafted an answer to one of the interview questions above, you can organise some 'speed-dating'-style interviews to discover more about potential group members and their positive attributes for your project team.

Consolidating the Project Team

The above exercises should help you to create the team for your media project. It is important to consolidate and analyse your newly formed team before embarking on any practical media work.

From our experience of working with student project teams, the following tips and hints will help you with this:

- Set deadlines and make a 'to-do' list to agree who needs to do what and when.
- Delegate tasks so each member has a role (or roles) and specific responsibilities.
- Try to establish a shared vision from the start. Vote and agree on a plan.
- Exchange contact details and keep in contact with each other using social media.
- Make sure everyone in the team contributes ideas early on so the team makes a good start.
- Assign a team leader to organise meetings and keep the group on track.
- Arrange regular team meetings and take minutes every time.
- Make sure everyone's voice is heard throughout the project.
- Assign specialist roles rather than having everyone do a bit of everything.

EXERCISE
Developing a Team Charter

A team charter should be developed to avoid the breakdown of the team and also to guide the team through the life of the project. You should be able to appoint a team leader from the results of investigating team dynamics earlier on in this chapter. Complete the team charter in Figure 2.3. Keep a record of the results of this discussion to refer to throughout the project.

Media Project Team Charter	
Context	
What is the purpose of the team?	
What is the problem the team needs to address?	
Aims and Objectives	
What is the main aim of the team?	
What are the main objectives of the team?	
Team Roles and Responsibilities	
Assign roles and responsibilities to each of the team members.	

(Continued)

Resources	
Itemise the resources available to the team, such as money, time, equipment, people, skills, knowledge, contacts.	
Organisation	
Describe how the team will organise itself. How often will they meet, when and where?	

FIGURE 2.3
Team charter form

Having produced a team charter, you should now turn your attention to agreeing on a team 'code of conduct'. It is important you do this at the outset so that the whole team understands the rules attached to the project work. This should help if there is a need for any conflict resolution and breakdown of the team in future. Start by discussing how you would like to operate as a successful group. Choose from the list below your priorities for a successful project team.

- Team members agree to stick to planned deadlines.
- Team members agree to discuss ideas within team meetings.
- Team members agree to show respect for each other's opinions, ideas throughout the project.
- Team members agree to attend all project meetings required and turn up on time.
- Team members agree to stay until the meeting or project work ends.
- Team members agree to give advance notice with good reason for being absent from team meetings and project work.
- Team members agree to share their ideas and skills when necessary.
- Team meetings will be guided by an agenda and minutes will be taken.
- Team members agree to complete their jobs on time.
- Team members agree not to attend to other business whilst engaged in a team meeting or media project work (for example, mobile phone or social media).
- Team members agree to support the team leader in their role.

Constructing Your Team Identity

Now that you have built your team for the practical media project and are ready to embark on the project it is time to construct your team's identity. This should assist the team in getting to know each other and begin to work effectively together. It will also have the effect of professionalising your practice.

EXERCISE
Team Identity

Team Name – decide on a name for your team. You might want to base this on the aspirations for the team that you have been discussing so far.

Team Photo – start to design your team's identity by taking a team photo as in Figure 2.4 below.

FIGURE 2.4
Production team photo

Team Logo – design a team logo. This should reflect the team's name and aspirations. This might be used in the credit sequence of a video, for example, or in any publicity you might produce at a later date. You could use a free logo design app available online for this.

Team Logo and Photo – this final image combines a team's logo and their group photo, which you could do.

FIGURE 2.5
Example of a production team's visual identity

Team Communication – now that you have established your team and its identity, spend some time setting up the following to enable team communication:

- Set up a group using your team's name on a chosen social media platform.
- Set up a shared folder using your team's name on a file-sharing cloud.
- Set up a team email account using your team's name.
- Set up a team group text using your team's name.
- Set up a team video-sharing account using your team's name.
- Set up a team blog using your team's name.

Team Meetings

Once you have your communications in place, you should also set up a routine for meeting as a team. Start this by deciding when the whole team is able to meet on a regular basis to discuss progress of the project. This meeting should be guided by an agenda as in the form in Figure 2.6. It is crucial that this is agreed now and all should look at diaries for the duration of the project identifying when they are free from other degree commitments, work shifts, holidays and so on. The meetings form should be completed during each meeting and a record kept in your file-sharing cloud. You could add this to a production log as evidence of effective teamwork.

Practical Media Project Team Meeting Minutes	
Name of team	
Date of meeting	
Time of meeting (start and end time)	
Location of meeting	
Names of team members present at the meeting	
Record of apologies for absence from the meeting	
Names of team members absent at the meeting (without apologies)	
Name of chair of the meeting	
Agenda (list of issues to discuss/things to do in the meeting)	Matters arising from the last meeting (with reference to the minutes from the last meeting)
	1.
	2.
	3.
	4. 5. etc. Any other business:

(Continued)

Agenda item (from agenda above)	Minutes (notes of discussion)	Action points (what needs to be done)	By whom? (who is responsible for doing what needs to be done)	By when? (date by which the task needs to be completed)
1.				
2.				
3.				
4.				
Date, time and location of next meeting				
End time of this meeting				

FIGURE 2.6
Form for team meetings

Summary

This chapter has been concerned with enabling you to establish an effective team for your practical media project work. It has provided a structure for you to consider your own role within a project team and to identify some of the associated skills required of you in many career areas. You should now have established the team for your project and you are ready to move on to establishing the brief. The focus of the next chapter is how to operate successfully as a team to satisfy a given project brief.

Further Reading

MindTools.com – this website is a very good resource for employability skills development. Although focused on business, it is applicable to an educational context and has some great resources for supporting teamwork and project management.

3

MEDIA PROJECT BRIEFS
From Media Student to Media Professional

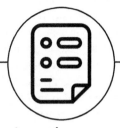

After reading this chapter you will be able to:

- establish the brief for your practical media project;
- consider media project work as part of ongoing work experience, and developing employability skills;
- develop project-management skills;
- communicate with brief providers or clients and manage your projects in a professional way.

Introduction

So far you have been engaged in building the project team and considering what skills are required for successful media group-project work. This chapter will help you consider how you might develop a professional approach to your practical work whilst at university. We will consider the different aspects of developing and working to project briefs with external organisations, thus working on projects in a professional client-based context.

Where to Find Project Briefs for a Media-Practice Project

Briefs for practical media projects can come from a variety of sources. This will depend on the course you are following, but broadly there are two types of project, the 'live brief' and the 'simulated brief'.

A simulated brief might be set by your tutor based on a theme such as examining particular issues or stories. These could perhaps be focused on such issues as citizenship, sustainability, university life and 'a day in the life of ...' for example. The brief provider then sets the theme, audience and market, media form and length.

A real or 'live' project brief, on the other hand, has great potential for genuine and deep experience in communication and project-management skills. This treats the student-based media project as a work-experience opportunity and has employability skills embedded. A real brief or live project will often be developed by your tutor, but you may also be involved in working up the project brief. This offers up many possibilities, as it is reflective of the corporate video industry, which you may end up working in on graduation. This sector is vast, especially when you take into account communications work for corporate clients, charities and the voluntary sector.

A project brief can be developed in many ways. You could look out for competitions and showcases which will provide a ready-made brief for a project. Charities often run competitions to produce media products for them based on a theme, so it is worth looking out for these. You could also look out for competitions and festivals online that you could use as the brief for your project work. Many of these festivals usually run on an annual basis and you can find more information in Chapter 10.

You could work with a department from your university and ask them to set you a brief for a media text that might be of use to them. This approach can be successful with the university marketing department, the alumni department, the sustainability department, the university outreach team, or perhaps your student union. Sometimes, the same brief provider might provide a number of briefs based on the same theme but each with a different focus (for example, audience/market/ subject, and so on).

The other source of project briefs is to look to external organisations in a variety of areas. The third sector is a rich resource for student media project briefs, as Harding points out:

> There are many community groups and campaign organisations with access to video equipment, but few that use them effectively ... The main reason is lack of purpose. Without purpose there is no strategy. Without strategy there is no social change. Without social change there is no video activism. (Harding, 2001: 15)

You could look in the not-for-profit, third sector, community and voluntary sectors. Most universities have a volunteering unit or department which will have a number of local organisations on its books for student volunteering. You could also look at volunteering websites.

You may also find contacts for a potential brief from within your project team. This may be a club or society that your fellow group members belong to, a hobby or interest they follow, or an organisation for which one of your team volunteers. It is best to avoid commercial projects for this type of brief to prevent undercutting those who work in the sector for their livelihood. It is also the case that once money and a profit motive is included, the educational basis of the project could get lost, so this type of project is best avoided.

Working Up a Project Brief

Whether your project brief is tutor or student generated will depend on many factors, such as the appropriateness to the curriculum and assessment criteria. It is important your tutor has some involvement in this process to help ensure the brief provider or client understands the commitment. However, negotiating your own brief can be a valuable part of the experience, with clear benefits for developing your employability.

Whatever the basis of your brief, it is important to work up a written form to ensure both client and project group have shared expectations about the project.

EXERCISE
Working Up Your Project Brief

Working in your media project team, create a briefing form using Figure 3.1. You should use the project briefing form as the basis of your first meeting. This should be re-visited on a regular basis throughout the project to ensure you are on-task with what is agreed.

Media Project Briefing Form		
Project Details		
Production team name		
Team leader name		
Production team contact details	Address	
	Email	
	Phone no.	
	Website	
	Social media sites	
Tutor's contact details	Address	
	Email	
	Phone no.	
	Website	
	Social media sites	

(Continued)

Brief provider/client details	Name of organisation	
	Name of main contact	
	Position in organisation	
	Address/postcode/directions for travel	
	Email	
	Phone no.	
	Website	
	Other forms of contact (social media sites, professional online profiles, cloud file-sharing sites, for example)	
Project briefing		
Preferred media form (video, photo exhibition, audio piece, website, etc.) Subject/theme of the media text		
Proposed content		
Proposed treatment/form (such as for video – documentary, infomercial, drama)		
Length/size of the media text		
Main aims for the production of the media text		
Deadline for completion of the project		
Schedule for the project (dates for pre-production, production, and post-production)		
Audience (primary audience, secondary audience)		

Market (where the media text will be shown, in what situations, to whom and why)		
Any other issues		
State any other issues related to this specific project that you feel are important before the project starts; for example: the need for safeguarding checks, the distance to travel for shooting and the nature of the organisation's service users		
Research sources		
Provide any sources that will help with the initial project research	Websites	
	Project reports and policy documents from the organisation	
	Archives	
	Face-to-face interviews	
	Action research such as job-shadowing, or work experience for the organisation	

FIGURE 3.1
Media project briefing form

Issues for the Brief Provider to Consider in Setting a Brief

If you are working with an external client, it is important you make them aware of the *educational context* of the project before you start. Setting and managing expectations around issues such as time commitment, available resources, levels of commitment and other constraints are very important in the early stages of the project. You should discuss the following considerations with your brief provider, whilst you are working up the project brief together:

- Establish that it is an educational project and as such the resulting quality may vary. The project could be treated in the same way as a work-experience placement might be. Give the brief provider the assessment criteria that will be used to assess the project (if available) and discuss these with them at the start.

- Discuss and agree the optimum size or length of the resulting project. Make sure it is manageable and realistic and relates to the requirements of the curriculum and resources (such

as time) available to you. You should agree to keep the brief tightly focused and avoid the temptation to cover everything for too wide an audience. Don't offer what you can't deliver!

- Make the brief provider aware that they as the client should offer their ideas for the project but that these ideas should not be too set in stone. Flexibility and creative freedom for the group will often result in a better project.

- Arrange regular meetings with the brief provider to discuss progress throughout. These meetings should be scheduled at the start of the project. Set up a clear system of communication. Agree on the method of communication (such as *just* through email, through texting, or through social media), and establish a main contact in the production team. Ask your brief provider to identify one main contact within their organisation. Agree that they will have the final say about the project to avoid 'too many cooks'.

- Give your brief provider a rough schedule for the project including dates of meetings, dates when the pre-production and research, production and post-production will be happening. Also make the brief provider aware of any times you are not available to work on the project (due to other modules' demands, exam and holiday dates, for example).

- Allow the brief provider to see a rough draft of the project for approval in good time for the deadline so that suggestions for changes can be made. Set a date for this in advance. Be clear about when the brief provider will receive the signed-off copy of the project, and in what format.

- Make the brief provider aware that it is the production team's responsibility to plan for, research and produce the project and to keep them updated on progress at regular intervals. Approval of the client should be sought through a script and storyboard meeting before production starts so a date for this should be set early on.

- Discuss the fact that it is the brief provider's responsibility to arrange the dates, times and places for shoots. They should organise safeguarding checks for the team if needed, and accompany the production team where necessary (especially where health and safety might be compromised). Your brief provider should usually arrange permissions for filming. For example, if any of their staff or service users appear in the video they will have to sign a consent form.

- You may need to negotiate with your brief provider to cover basic expenses such as transport costs. If so, do this at the start of the project and find out the process for claiming expenses back. Let your brief provider know that you are required to use copyright-free material in the project and that if they wish to use anything else, the copyright clearance will be their responsibility.

Dreams and Nightmares for Successful Media Project Work

Now that you have set up your project brief it is a good idea to take a little time to think about what you want to achieve from the project. Thinking ahead like this is a useful way of

approaching projects and a useful employability skill. It will also help you when it comes to reflecting on the project at the end.

EXERCISE
Dreams and Nightmares for Practical Media Project Work

Now that you have established your production team, and have analysed the necessary skills and experience required to make a good team, identify your hopes and fears for the practical media project you are about to embark on. Create a table like the one in Figure 3.2. Discuss the results of this exercise with your production team and remind yourselves about the strategies in column 3 throughout the project.

	Hopes/dreams for the project	Fears/nightmares for the project	Strategy for realising dreams and avoiding the nightmares
1.	**Example:** Complete an impressive film that our client is happy with and uses in future	**Example:** Disappointing our brief provider by not fulfilling the brief and the video not being signed off	**Example:** Communicate with our brief provider, keeping them up to date with our progress at all times. Show rough drafts throughout and ask for regular feedback
2.			
3.			
4.			
5.			

FIGURE 3.2
Dreams and nightmares for practical media project work

Thinking about Stakeholders for the Project

Thinking about what you want to gain from the experience of doing a media-practice project is important as part of your preparation work. You should think about and identify what each of the stakeholders for the project stand to gain from it, and what risks may be inherent in it. Being aware of this before you start work will help you to realise that it is not just *you* and *your group* who have vested interests in the project. It is important to recognise that the motivations of each stakeholder will be different, and will have a different impact upon the success of the project. The following exercise will help you to recognise the risks and rewards for each of the stakeholders involved in your project.

EXERCISE
Thinking about Stakeholders

Using the form in Figure 3.3, identify what each of the stakeholders for your project stands to gain from its success. In each of the relevant columns, make a list of possible gains and risks for each of the stakeholders. In the final column develop a strategy to ensure that each stakeholder has maximum gains from the project.

Stakeholder	Gains	Risks	Strategies
Your production team	Example: Work experience and social and cultural awareness.	Example: Not understanding the needs of the client's organisation.	Example: Treat the project like a real 'live' brief, rather than a simulation.
The project brief provider/client			
The project brief provider's service users			
Your university/degree course			
Your tutor			

FIGURE 3.3
Thinking about stakeholders

Revisit the results of this exercise throughout the project to stay focused and keep in mind the requirements of each of the stakeholders. You can use this to inform your detailed setting up of the project.

Project Management for a Successful Media Project

Now that you have set up your project brief and determined who your brief provider/client will be, you are ready to get started with the project. Using some basic management techniques for your media-practice project will be useful for the project itself, but will also provide some valuable employability skills for your future career. In relation to your media-practice project, you should begin with the research and development phase by initiating the project. This could involve the development of a project requirement analysis as below.

Media-Project Requirement Analysis

Any project produced for a client should start by clearly agreeing what you will actually deliver. You have already worked up or been given a detailed project brief. Now you should have a go at analysing and agreeing exactly what it is you will deliver as a result of the project. A media-project requirement analysis can help you to avoid problems of mis-matching expectations between you and your brief provider. This can help avoid common problems such as the brief provider complaining it's not what they asked for; having a change of mind halfway through the project; conflicting needs from several different stakeholders; failing to deliver the whole project; and so on.

EXERCISE
Preparing a Media-Project Requirement Analysis

Complete the project analysis in Figure 3.4 with your media-project group. This should be completed after the project brief has been agreed, with all the project stakeholders present.

Identify the stakeholders for the project
Who is the project's brief provider?
Identify the stakeholders' requirements for the project
What does the project brief provider want and expect from the project?
What does the project's audience want and expect from the project?
Definition: describe the basic idea and the background to the project.

(Continued)

Purpose: describe why you are doing the project.

Objectives: list some specific objectives for the project and describe how success will be measured.

Scope: describe the scope of the project, for example, type of work, type of client, type of issue.

Deliverables: describe what will be delivered as a result of the project.

Constraints: list and describe any constraints that could affect the success of the project.

Benefits: describe the benefits of the project and how these will be measured.

Resources: give a breakdown of the project resources such as equipment, time and transport.

Schedule: give a detailed schedule for the project. Identify a timetable for the pre-production, production and post-production phases, and list deadline dates.

Risks: identify and describe any potential risks within the project.

Plan B: describe how you will avoid the risks identified above.

Project jobs: list the major jobs that need to be completed during the project.

Human resources: list the team to work on the project, identify the roles of each team member, estimate the amount of time each team member will need to give to the project.

FIGURE 3.4
Media-project requirement analysis

Discuss and agree the contents of this form with your project brief provider. You should revisit the results of your analysis throughout the project to ensure you are on target.

Working with External Clients/Brief Providers

So far you have initiated your project and agreed with your brief provider the scope and nature of it. You are now ready to build a professional relationship with your client. Here is some advice about working with external brief providers on university-based media projects:

- Have a team leader who is the sole communicator with the brief provider. This is an efficient way for the client to share information with the team and be involved.

- Exchange email address and phone numbers. Create an email address under the production team's name purely for the purpose of contacting the brief provider.

- Listen to the client's ideas and keep them up to date with the project. If you listen to their ideas they are more likely to appreciate the final product.

- Get to know your brief provider's organisation. Visit several times before embarking on the production, and perhaps volunteer for the organisation.

- Always take notes during meetings in order to ensure you achieve what the brief provider wants the project to accomplish.

- Ensure deadlines are known. Allow your brief provider to know all deadlines and vice versa so everyone understands the time constraints of the project.

- Use social media as a tool for showing the brief provider drafts of your work.

- Be professional when contacting and meeting your brief provider. You want them to take you seriously and it is important to show that you are committed to the project.

Professionalism

The advice given above has established how best to work with an external client on a university-based media project. Such a project based on a real issue/topic and briefed by a real client, external to the university, is an excellent opportunity to develop your professionalism. Professionalism is an important skill to learn and practise, and a university media project is the perfect safe space to develop these skills that will be important for your future career.

Client-led media projects can be seen as an ongoing work experience opportunity, and contribute directly to your CV. Professionalism is important whilst working within your project team and whilst working with your client/brief provider. Emotional intelligence in the (work-experience) workplace is the basis of professionalism.

According to Daniel Goleman (2004) there are five basic features of emotional intelligence:

- **Self-awareness**: the ability to understand your own strengths and weaknesses.
- **Self-regulation**: the ability to think before acting, having openness to change and having the ability to say 'no'.
- **Internal motivation**: a genuine reason or passion for acting or behaving in a particular way. Having the ability to defer immediate results for the benefit of receiving long-term gains.
- **Social skills**: the personal skills needed for successful communication and interaction. Being good at building and maintaining relationships.
- **Empathy**: the ability to understand the feelings of others.

Emotional intelligence is important because it enables you to see how others might see you, and helps you to behave appropriately in professional situations.

Imagine, for example, how you might react if one of your teammates (or a work colleague) were to behave in the following ways:

- Refuses to do jobs that are not directly linked to their media production or area of technical skill.
- Words their emails in sloppy or inappropriate ways.
- Uses their mobile phone at inappropriate times.
- Complains of being too tired due to previous late nights.
- Does not turn up or is late, with no apology or explanation to production meetings.
- Spends lots of work time on social media and makes no attempt to hide it.
- Makes no attempt to disguise a full open-mouthed yawn during team meetings.
- Only turns up when it suits them.
- Chats, giggles and smirks whilst others are talking in meetings.
- Complains about a brief that they have been set as being beneath them or boring.

You can appreciate that all of the above would seem highly inappropriate in a professional work situation, but you have probably witnessed this type of behaviour on some occasions – maybe in a lecture, or during group work – from one of your peers! Now is the perfect opportunity to develop a sense of self-awareness. You could practise treating the *university workplace* like a *professional workplace*, especially in the context of your media project work. This is the basis of having emotional intelligence.

As part of their research into employability and graduate identity, Geoffrey Hinchliffe and Adrienne Jolley (2010) list the many expectations that employers have of graduates. The words in bold below highlight the skills where emotional intelligence (defined above) is important and these are areas you might like to prioritise for future development. Think about how close you are to displaying these attributes, and think of examples of times your peers (or you!) might have contradicted them:

- demonstrates **honesty** and **integrity**;
- is **trustworthy**;
- is able to **listen** to others;
- is able to **integrate** quickly into a **team** or department;
- is able to **present ideas** clearly, both verbally and in writing;
- demonstrates good **time-management**;
- can demonstrate attention to **detail** and **thoroughness**;
- has a **mature** attitude;
- is willing to take **responsibility** for their own work;
- can **share** ideas with others;
- can demonstrate **tact**;
- demonstrates **social/cultural awareness**;
- is able to take the **initiative**;
- can be **relied upon** by other members of the team/department;
- is willing to take on new **challenges** and **responsibilities**;
- thinks **critically** about their work.

You can see how the keywords highlighted in bold above are personal skills linked to emotional intelligence and professional behaviour, and not to technical prowess! If you refer back to the 'Group-Project Dynamics and Individual Characteristics' section in Chapter 2, you will notice that the 'Very Good' and 'First-Class Teamworker' categories possess many of the positive traits of emotional intelligence given above. These personal skills are transferable and can be developed during your media-practice projects, and subsequently applied to your future career. The next exercise will enable you to focus on what constitutes professional and unprofessional behaviour.

EXERCISE
Professional and Unprofessional Behaviour

In order to maintain professional behaviour, it helps to predict a series of 'worst-case scenarios' so that you can plan to avoid unprofessional behaviour taking place during your own media-practice projects.

Look at the list of potentially unprofessional situations outlined below. These are all scenarios that are commonplace in student-based media projects. Reflect on one occasion from your previous work experience or team-project work, where similar incidents have occurred. Draw up a strategy to make sure you avoid these incidents happening in your project work.

Scenario	Strategy to avoid this scenario happening to you
Rumour and gossip One of your teammates gossips about a colleague or client and it comes back to haunt them! The person they bitched to assumes this is how they speak about them too, behind their back. Consequently, your teammate loses all respect.	
Social media You create a group chat to support your project, but a colleague ends up posting inappropriate updates about their social life instead!	
Over-sensitivity A teammate takes criticism about their work and contribution to the project too personally. They do not understand that someone is trying to give them constructive advice in order to improve their work.	
Punctuality Someone in your group is often late to production meetings. They get the reputation for being unreliable which they then find hard to shake off, even when they put the effort into improving their timekeeping.	
Mobile phone over-dependence A team member spends much of their project work time paying more attention to their phone. As a result, their teammates think that they lack commitment.	
Email etiquette Someone in your group lacks email etiquette; for example, they send emails to the client in the middle of the night and badger them for an immediate response. They use casual language and ignore accepted email protocol. This reflects badly on the project group.	

Emotional excess A team member's self-obsession with their emotional state interferes with the progress of the project. For example, the teammate lets people know that they are bored/hungover/hungry/grumpy/heartbroken/anxious/stressed. This slows the project down.	
Unrealistic goals Your team promises your client too much from the project, and subsequently can't deliver by the agreed deadline. This tarnishes the professional reputation of the group.	

FIGURE 3.5
Avoiding unprofessional behaviour

Summary

In this chapter we have discussed how to find and set up briefs for your projects. You have developed a range of project-management skills. As well as being useful for your work at university, these will be transferable to a variety of employment contexts. You have also considered ways of working constructively and professionally with your team on client-led briefs. In the next chapter we will be looking at the important areas of audiences and audience research.

Further Reading

To deepen your understanding about emotional intelligence in the workplace, have a look at Daniel Goleman's book:

Goleman, Daniel, 2004, *Emotional Intelligence and Working with Emotional Intelligence*, London: Bloomsbury Publishing.

To find out more about what employers are looking for from graduates search online for the following:

Hinchliffe, Geoffrey, and Jolley, Adrienne, Hecsu.ac.uk – graduate market trends, spring 2010.

4

REACHING YOUR AUDIENCE
Media Practice, Production and Consumption

After reading this chapter you will be able to:

- make links between analytical approaches to audience research, and practical methods of audience research;
- understand how potential audiences will respond to your work;
- conduct audience research using a broad variety of methods;
- compose questionnaires and surveys.

Introduction

In the previous chapter we discussed how to set up a project brief. This chapter will consider the audience for your media projects. Audience research is an important aspect of professional industry practice. Production companies and broadcasters use audience research in order to determine if their product will appeal to consumers. Therefore, the identification of an audience for a particular project of yours is crucial.

Take for example, the idea of production aesthetics, cultural contexts and taste preferences. These should be considered in the early stages of pre-production when you are researching and defining your audience. The style of any type of media production – be it video, web design or advertising – is largely dictated by audience tastes and preferences, and this will have an effect on the way that you design and construct your own productions.

As a media-practice student, it is useful for you to understand analytical approaches to audience research that can then be applied to your own work. A greater understanding of this research will ensure that you analyse a suitable sample size and a relevant demographic, and most importantly that you avoid making assumptions about the audience.

In this chapter we are interested in looking at how audiences respond to, and use, texts in different ways. This in turn will help you to think about how audiences might potentially respond to, and consume, your work. Useful models for your projects will be uses and gratifications research and ethnographic research. First, however, we will start by considering the ways that texts are encoded and decoded.

Encoding and Decoding

Considering the audience raises the question of how media texts come to have meaning. Meanings in texts are not only produced at the point of *production*, but also at the point of *consumption*. In other words, audiences can construct meaning in texts by the way that they interpret them. A useful piece of research to refer to here is that done by Stuart Hall on 'encoding and decoding'. Hall argues that before a message can have meaning, it must first be meaningfully decoded. In other words, it must be understood or interpreted by the audience.

Hall argues that the 'sender/message/receiver' model of communication is too simplistic, that it supposes that the receiver of the message is passive and will interpret the message in exactly the way that the producer intended it to be read (Hall, 1999: 51). There may be any number of factors that affect interpretation, from differences in cultural tastes to levels of education.

On first assumption we might think that the production of your media text and its interpretation is very straightforward. For example, you produce a video, it is posted online, then watched and understood by the viewer. However, meaning can be affected at all three points of construction: production, distribution and reception, and these all have a bearing on how your text is understood.

Perhaps your audience does not like watching your video because the mode of address is too serious; perhaps they watch your comedy film and laugh in all the wrong places!

In order to demonstrate how audience readings may differ, Stuart Hall suggests there are three hypothetical models of decoding (interpreting) a text:

1. A dominant-hegemonic position – the audience member accepts the intended or preferred meaning.
2. A negotiated code – the audience member takes on the preferred meaning but this is also tempered by 'oppositional' positions according to the cultural and social contexts of the reader.
3. An oppositional code – the preferred interpretation of the media text or message is understood but rejected by its consumer.

Encoding and decoding demonstrates that not all audiences are the same. It highlights the *active* role that audiences play in the process of media consumption, and dispels the myth of the *passive* viewer.

EXERCISE
Dominant–Negotiated–Oppositional Codes

Analysing other people's work for dominant–negotiated–oppositional codes can help you to think about how you construct meaning in your own projects, and whether you are successfully identifying your audience.

Choose three student video projects to analyse. These can be anything, from a piece of fiction, a documentary or a client-led information video. The form and genre is not important. Analyse the three videos by using the following questions as a guide, and discuss your personal responses with a group of your peers:

- What do you think the main purpose of the video is? (Is it to entertain or to inform?)
- Who do you think the intended audience is? Fellow students? An external client? Fans of a particular genre (for example, comedy, horror, social realism)?
- How do you know who the intended audience is? (Are there clues such as character types in the video for the audience to relate to?)
- Is the mode of address formal or informal?
- Were you entertained by the video?
- Have you learned anything from watching the video?
- Did the video 'speak' to you as an audience member?
- Did you identify with the video in any way?

Now analyse your responses. Were there any disagreements amongst the group about any of the above points, or did you all tend to respond to the video in the same way? How would you rate each peer's response to the videos following Hall's model:

- dominant;
- negotiated;
- oppositional?

Now ask yourselves why you think you responded to the videos in these ways:

- If the video 'spoke' to you as an audience member, why do you think this was?
- If you identified with the video, why do you think this was?

Uses and Gratifications

'Uses and gratifications' involves 'real' audience members as part of research, and acknowledges how they make use of different types of media in different ways to suit different needs. When conducting audience research, you should ask your audience about their views and why they use media, rather than making assumptions about their viewing and listening habits.

Uses and gratifications theory considers audiences more as individuals, rather than as a passive, undifferentiated 'mass', and explores how they actively use texts. Denis McQuail's early research into uses and gratifications was arranged into these four typologies:

- diversion: entertainment, escape from routine or problems, emotional release;

- personal relationships: integration, shared interests, social interaction;

- personal identity: self-reference, personal value reinforcement;

- surveillance: for seeking information, learning about the world.

(McQuail, 2010: 424)

Let's apply this theory to a practical exercise.

EXERCISE
Uses and Gratifications in Popular Music

A uses and gratifications analysis can be applied to any audio-visual texts including feature films, drama series, websites, and so on. It is an interesting way of finding out how and why audience members use a particular form of media. You could try some research like this prior to producing a media project of your own. This exercise focuses on popular music.

Interview one of your peers about their favourite band/musician/singer. Ask them the following questions:

- Who is your favourite band/musician/singer?
- What is your favourite song of theirs?
- When do you listen to the band/musician/singer?
- Why do you enjoy listening to them?
- How does their music make you feel?
- How do you relate to the lyrics?
- Do you have friends who listen to the same band/musician/singer?
- Have you been to a gig/concert with your friends to see the band/musician/singer?
- Do you own any merchandise (T-shirts, posters) relating to the band/musician/singer?
- Has the band/musician/singer inspired you to play/record music of your own?

Consider how these questions are framed so that they are directed *to* and involve the interviewee. Consider the contexts in which the music is listened, why they enjoy it, and the effects that the music has on his or her life. Now analyse the answers using the following model in order to find out how the audience member 'uses' the band/musician/singer:

- diversion;
- personal relationships;
- personal identity;
- surveillance.

Using Questionnaires for Audience Research

Questionnaires are one of the most frequently used methods of audience research conducted by student project groups. However, these are often not constructed well enough to elicit meaningful results. The next exercise will give you the chance to practise composing and using questionnaires for your research.

EXERCISE
Practising Using a Questionnaire

The example in Figure 4.1 is about student radio audiences: who listens to student radio, and what their listening tastes are. It also aims to find out when audience members listen to particular programmes at particular times of the day. Use the questionnaire below to interview your peers about student radio. Note how the questions have a logical structure. To ensure the results are useful, you should aim to get as large a sample size as you can. This should be possible given your access to a large population of students and through the use of social media for distribution. The respondents should be reassured that they will remain anonymous. They should be allowed to withdraw from the questionnaire or survey at any point during the questioning.

	Question	Answer
1	What gender are you?	M/F/prefer not to say
2	What age group are you?	16–22 23–29 30–39 40 plus Prefer not to say
3	What nationality are you?	
4	What course are you studying?	
5	Do you listen to the radio?	Yes/No
6	If yes, what type of station do you listen to?	Student radio BBC radio Commercial radio
7	How many hours per day/week/month do you listen to the radio?	Every day 2–3 days per week 1 day per week 2–3 days per month 1 day per month

(Continued)

	Question	Answer
8	What time/s of day do you listen to the radio?	Morning Lunchtime Afternoon Evening Night
9	Do you listen to the station for any of the following:	Music News (current affairs) News (local/social updates) Sports updates Quizzes Drama Other (please state)
10	What particular show/s do you listen to?	
11	What attracts you to this show/these shows?	Content Presenter Time of day Other reason (please state)
12	Do you follow the station's social media accounts?	Yes/No If Yes: Twitter Facebook Other (please state)
13	Have you ever interacted with the station?	Yes/No If Yes: Requested a song Phoned in Taken part in a quiz Appeared on air as a presenter Appeared on air as an interviewee Other (please state)
14	What type of show would you like to listen to that isn't currently on air?	
15	Would you be willing to take part in a focus group discussion or interview? If so, please leave your contact details.	

FIGURE 4.1
Audience research questionnaire

Once you have a satisfactory sample of responses, you should analyse the results to find out what shows people listen to at particular times, which shows are most popular, if there is a gap in the market, and so on. Analyse the results by saying why you think the station's existing formula is successful, or what improvements could be made to the station.

Now analyse the answers to the questions using the following 'uses and gratifications' model in order to find out how the audience member 'uses' the radio station:

- diversion: entertainment, escape from routine or problems, emotional release;
- personal relationships: integration, shared interests, social interaction;
- personal identity: self-reference, personal value reinforcement;
- surveillance: for seeking information, learning about the world.

Try analysing the results in different ways to find out more information about the audience demographic; for example using:

- gender;
- year of study;
- degree subject.

You can see from the way the questions are designed in the questionnaire above how much information can potentially be extracted from such a piece of research. You can now adapt the previous model to research the audience for your own media projects.

A questionnaire is useful for gathering quantitative research, but you could follow this up with some qualitative research by asking respondents if they would like to be interviewed further about their listening tastes, or to take part in a focus-group discussion. We will now consider how you could conduct qualitative research as a follow-up to quantitative research.

Audiences and Ethnographic Research

We have looked at how uses and gratifications research considers the audience's needs, and the audience's own opinions about the ways that they use media. One of the problems with conducting interactive audience research of this kind, however, is that during qualitative research-like interviews and focus groups researchers cannot always rely on what audience members tell them as being completely honest. There is always the possibility that interviewees will tell researchers what they think they want them to hear! In order to gain a clear understanding of the ways in which media is used, detailed research into media and cultural studies also has to take into account social, historical and political contexts. This is where ethnographic research comes into use.

Ethnographic research can be carried out using a combination of observing participants, writing notes, and then analysing the observation according to social orientation or viewing contexts.

As with all methods of research, there are pros and cons with each of the above, especially if the environment in which observation takes place is not natural to the persons being observed, or if the presence of the researcher alters the way the participants talk or behave.

EXERCISE
Practise Using Quantitative and Qualitative Methods

This is a practical exercise, involving a focus-group discussion which follows the previous questionnaire exercise about student radio. This will provide more in-depth research when gathering data.

Focus Group

Analyse the results of your questionnaire and see if there are any particular responses that could be developed and analysed further. Once you have identified some areas of the topic that require further discussion, then you should organise a focus group. In a group of approximately six people (for example with four talking and two taking notes), carry out a focus-group discussion of the topic you conducted the questionnaire about.

It may be a good idea to record the session on your phone, or film the focus group, but make sure you obtain written consent from the participants before recording them. Recording and taking notes is a good idea because it covers all eventualities – there may be nuances that you miss during a recording, and the note-takers can compare their notes. Similarly, if you cannot write everything down, the recording will provide you with a back-up.

Limit the discussion to between five and ten minutes. You can use some prompt questions to get the discussion started, and to help shape it if the group goes too far off-topic.

Once you have gathered your research data, you should use the quantitative data (questionnaire results) to construct statistics, tables and pie charts, and the qualitative data (focus-group results) to provide further analytical depth.

For the qualitative data, do not simply describe the results, but ask questions such as:

- Why did the members of the focus group have this opinion?
- Can any of the results be explained by historical and social contexts such as gender, ethnicity, age range, year of study, degree subject, and so on?
- Were the methods of research carried out satisfactorily?
- Could peer pressure have influenced some of the responses?
- What aspects of the research worked well?
- How could the methods of research be improved upon?

Write a short report about your research project, and make sure that you use this research effectively in order to inform your project. Whenever audience research is required of your project work you should revisit this methodology.

Audience Research in Practice

Whatever methods you use to gather data, you should aim to be as rigorous as possible, and to gather results that are valid. There is very little point in doing research for a project with respondents who are not appropriate to the media text – for example conducting a survey with a handful of friends, when the media text is a client-led project for elderly service users of a local charity!

The following section of this chapter will help you to practise and refine conducting audience research.

Quantitative research conducted via online questionnaires can be useful if you want to maintain objectivity and the respondents' anonymity, but the size of the audience sample might also be significant for this type of research. You need to get a large sample size in order for the qualitative data to be meaningful and significant. If using online surveys, make sure the questions are quick to answer. Busy respondents can be put off if they have to spend too long filling in questionnaires. Instead, try using multiple-choice questions, or answers structured on a scale of 1 to 5 (strongly agree, agree, don't know, disagree, strongly disagree). If you have difficulty gathering data via online surveys, then it is best to produce hard copies and approach people in person.

As outlined previously in this chapter, it can be useful to combine methods of quantitative and qualitative research; quantitative to gather data such as 'how many and who?', and qualitative to gather data such as 'why, when and how?'

Composing Questions for Audience Research

Effective audience research comes through practice. The more you practise writing questions and analysing the results, the better you will become at conducting your research. It takes some skill to write questions that will garner satisfactory results, and in order to do this you should try to avoid writing 'closed' or 'leading' questions, or questions that may make the respondent feel uncomfortable, and therefore halt the line of questioning. For example, imagine you are conducting some research regarding drama series viewing habits. How do the following questions compare?

1. Are you a regular viewer of [the drama series]?
2. How regularly do you watch [the drama series]? Frequently/occasionally/never

The first question will garner a 'yes' or 'no' answer, and therefore does not give you a satisfactory answer with much depth. The second question, however, will provide you with more detail, because the respondent is being invited to tell you how often they watch the programme. Now compare the next two questions:

1. Who is your favourite character?
2. Are there any particular characters on the programme that stand out? If so, why?

The first question only asks them to name one character that they like, but does not ask why they like them. The second question, however, asks if there are any characters that stand out and why – it does not lead the respondent to only talk about a character that they like. Therefore, they could reply either positively or negatively, by talking about characters that they like, dislike or find amusing, for instance.

Finally, have a look at the next two questions:

1. Tell me about a funny storyline from the drama series, or something that shocked you.
2. Are there any memorable incidents/storylines in [the drama series] that made an impact on you? Explain why.

The first example is a leading question, because it mentions two possible emotional responses (amusement and shock), whereas the second version asks the respondent to refer to any storyline that is memorable. The second question also asks the respondent to elaborate by explaining why they reacted in such a way.

EXERCISE
Composing Interview Questions

Imagine that the following set of questions have been composed to find out about audience tastes in film stars, and how audiences might relate to film stars for inspiration in their daily lives.

Try out the following list of questions on a group of your peers, and record the results.

1. Who is your favourite film star?
2. How long have you liked them?
3. What is your favourite film of theirs?
4. Are they good at acting?
5. Do you like them because you think they are good-looking?
6. Have they appeared in a number of different film genres?
7. Do they provide you with inspiration?

Have a go at *rewriting* the questions in order to gather more satisfactory, in-depth results. You should also add some control questions to record gender, ethnicity, levels of education and age range, for example, to determine whether these have an effect on the respondents' tastes, as we have mentioned previously. What kind of responses did the original questions garner? How do the responses to your rewritten questions compare?

By comparing and contrasting the results, you should be able to see how important it is to word your questions carefully to avoid getting unsatisfactory results such as 'yes' or 'no' answers. Think carefully about the aims of each question, and how you are going to use the results. Once you have practised writing interview questions you can apply this skill to some real audience research for your own projects.

Tips and Hints about Doing Audience Research

- It is always important to identify the audience at the start of any project.
- Never take your audience for granted.
- If using online questionnaires, make sure the questions are quick to answer.
- Try distributing your questionnaires via appropriate channels – for example, online fan communities who will forward your surveys to other fans, causing a snowball effect.
- Use a combination of methods to gather data: quantitative followed by qualitative.

Summary

In this chapter we have introduced you to ways of thinking about how your media projects can connect with real-life audiences, and how you need to seriously consider the audience during the planning stages of your work. You will now be able to make connections between theoretical approaches to audiences and use this to inform your own media practice.

In the following chapter, we also make connections between theory and practice, by looking at different approaches to narrative theory that can enhance your skills in writing and narrative construction.

Further Reading

For a general insight into audience research and communication theory we recommend that you read the following:

Hall, Stuart, 1999, 'Encoding and Decoding' in During, Simon (ed.), *The Cultural Studies Reader*, London: Routledge.

McQuail, Denis, 2010, *McQuail's Mass Communication Theory*, 6th edition, London: Sage.

McQuail, Denis, Blumler, Jay G., and Brown, J. R., 1999, 'The Television Audience: A Revised Perspective' in Marris, Paul and Thornham, Sue (eds), *Media Studies: A Reader*, Edinburgh: Edinburgh University Press.

5

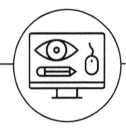

SCRIPTING YOUR PROJECTS
Ideas, Forms and Genres

After reading this chapter you will be able to:

- develop your writing skills for a variety of different media forms including fiction and non-fiction;
- apply theories of genre and narrative to your own practical projects;
- pitch your storytelling ideas and respond to feedback;
- transform your scripts into storyboard images.

Introduction

The previous chapter helped you to research the potential audience for your media projects. This chapter will now enable you to consider how to script your own work. It will include guided exercises to spark ideas, and support the writing and storyboarding of your work for fiction and non-fiction products.

One of the aims of this chapter is not simply to advise you 'how to' write but, rather, to think about why you are writing, the contexts of your writing, the effects that this will have in relation to the rest of your work and how it communicates with your audience. Writing for audio-visual media is a useful employability skill to develop. These skills are useful, even if you do not intend to become a 'screenwriter' in the media and creative industries. Skills in writing are covered by a variety of jobs including copywriting, speech writing, writing for marketing and advertising campaigns, and so on. Therefore, skills in understanding and interpreting writing – of differing forms, such as documentaries, interviews and fictional screenplays – will stand you in good stead for a wide variety of careers.

Ideas

The first hurdle to jump with any project is coming up with your initial idea. One of the benefits of working on a student project – which is similar to professional practice – is that you will usually be given a project brief that you are required to fulfil. In many respects this shares a common ground with your future employment. Almost everything you write or produce during your career will be made for a client, and even if you produce a short video for a film festival, the festival will often have a specific theme or genre that the entries are required to follow.

No idea that anyone comes up with will be completely original, but this should not put you off! If you are struggling to find ideas, then you should look around for some inspiration from other sources such as poems, news stories or real-life events.

At the early stage of a project you should make a note of any ideas that come into your head. Do not reject any ideas! This will prevent inertia and it will also enable you to discuss several ideas with your tutor or peers before making a final decision. However, you should aim to keep your ideas simple and focused. Students often try to cram too many complex ideas into one project, when simplicity would serve them better! Overthinking can also sometimes inhibit progress.

Pilar Alessandra, author of *The Coffee Break Screenwriter*, convinces us that a screenwriter only needs a ten-minute deadline to write a great idea for a screenplay. If they are given an additional ten minutes they 'overwrite. They think too much. They fix what ain't broke, and they write themselves into a corner' (Alessandra, 2010: xi). Paul Ashton reminds us that the best film stories have universal appeal and 'translate across languages, countries, territories and continents' (Ashton, 2011: 32). An audience must be able to understand and connect with what you are trying to communicate, and this is why the best narratives are often based upon the simplest of concepts.

Speed-writing is the best way to get yourself started on any writing assignment – not just a screenplay. It is always best to put some words down on paper or on your computer rather than stare at a blank screen. This is why the ten-minute screenwriting exercise is a useful transferable skill. You can treat whatever you write as a first draft, and go back to it later, after a break, to fine-tune it.

EXERCISE
Looking for Inspiration

This exercise aims to test your skills in storytelling and to help you develop ideas into a fully fledged project.

You are given a brief to start a new project. The project requires you to write a short script or to come up with an idea that will be turned into a short film. In order to brainstorm some ideas, ask yourself the following questions about a story that you heard today:

- What was the first story you consumed this morning?
- Where did you read about or hear the story?
- Was it a big event, or a piece of gossip more close to home?

- How many people did it involve?
- Where did it happen?
- When did it happen?
- Over what time frame did it happen?
- How did the story begin and end?
- Was it an amusing story with a punchline?
- Was it a sad story that ended with an element of pathos or hope?

Write a short summary of the story, quickly and succinctly – in no more than 10 minutes.

The above exercise will get your storytelling juices flowing! They will confirm your storytelling skills and make you consider what the main elements of any story are, however inconsequential the story may seem. If the story did make an impact on you then you could consider adapting it for one of your projects.

Genre

So far, we have given you some tips and hints about how and where to find ideas. We now need to add some depth to these ideas, and in order to do this it may help to start thinking of your work in terms of genre and narrative. We will spend the next few pages discussing writing for fictional forms. Later in the chapter this will be followed by examining writing for non-fiction.

Genre – from the French word for types or kinds – is a useful way of pigeonholing or categorising media texts into recognisable and easily identifiable forms, and the term will be familiar to all film studies and media students.

The pleasures that audiences derive from genre films come from a certain extent due to an element of familiarity, and this is why genre films are often a popular reference point for student productions. When most student project groups are brainstorming ideas for a short video, they will often describe their ideas in terms of genre, saying they are going to make a 'comedy' or a 'horror film'. You might want to test your familiarity with genre conventions, by carrying out the following exercise. The important thing to note here is that genre conventions are often very focused and can be narrowed down to a few simple elements or motifs.

EXERCISE
Identifying Genre Conventions in Film

Identify the following film genres by recognising their conventions of setting, character, time period and style of music.

	SETTING	CHARACTERS	TIME PERIOD	STYLE OF MUSIC	GENRE
1	USA, empty Victorian house, built in the Gothic Revival style	A group of teenagers	1980s	Synthesisers	Horror film in the 'slasher' sub-genre
2	Inner city, centred around the workplace or factory	Working-class British	1960s	Jazz score	Social realism
3	Stately home, English countryside	Extended family of aristocrats and their servants	Edwardian era	Classical	British heritage genre

FIGURE 5.1
Identifying genre conventions in film

Think up some genre conventions of your own, and quiz some of your peers. Try to be as obscure and inventive as you can be in order to test your peers' knowledge of genre and genre conventions, and to see how the essence of a piece of fiction can be condensed into these few simple elements.

Narrative Structure

Narratives are often considered in the form of a linear, chronological, three-act structure: the beginning, middle and end. The three-act structure can be applied to even the simplest of texts and appears like this:

1. exposition: an introduction to the setting, main characters and situation;
2. complication: the situation is compromised in some way, the hero/heroine is confronted with a challenge;
3. climax and denouement: the complication is resolved, the story reaches a conclusion.

However, Tzvetan Todorov's theory of the five-act narrative structure takes this further. Rather than looking at a three-act structure, Todorov argues that narrative goes through a transformation of cause and effect in five stages, which are:

1. a state of equilibrium at the outset;
2. a disruption of the equilibrium by some action;
3. a recognition that there has been a disruption;
4. an attempt to repair the situation;
5. a reinstatement of the initial equilibrium.

Stages 3 and 4 add an extra dimension to the middle 'complication' stage of the three-act structure. Not only has there been a 'disruption' (stage 2), but this disruption is recognised, and the hero or heroine then attempts to restore the equilibrium. As Todorov explains, 'the second equilibrium [stage 5] is similar to the first, but the two are never identical' (Todorov cited in Cohen and Shires, 1997: 54).

EXERCISE
Structuring Your Project According to Todorov's Theory

This exercise will help you start to develop a piece of fictional work. Referring to a storyline you developed in the exercises above, summarise the narrative according to Todorov's five-part structure.

Explain each of the following in no more than 20 words:

- equilibrium;
- disruption of equilibrium;
- recognition of disruption;
- attempt to repair disruption;
- reinstatement of initial equilibrium.

Seven Parameters for Storytelling in the Short Fiction Film

One aspect that most student videos have in common is that they are relatively short. Richard Raskin argues that when short fiction films are 'at their best, they tell stories with such remarkable economy that they take our breath away' (Raskin, 2002: 1). He points to seven parameters for story design in short fiction films that focus on depth of meaning and economy of style. These seven parameters are a useful tool for analysing your own work, but as Raskin argues, these should be seen as 'an option for enhancing the storytelling values of a film' rather than a 'condition for good story design' and that a film need not necessarily contain all seven schemata (Raskin, 2002: 165). He sees the seven schemata as follows:

1. character focus and character interaction: 'letting the viewer know whose story is being told, yet counteracting the risk of static portraiture by keeping the main character(s) interacting';
2. causality and choice: 'making cause and effect relationships central to the story, but having the causality flow from the main character's deliberate choices';
3. consistency and surprise: 'keeping behaviour consistent with each character's definition, yet utterly unpredictable';
4. image and sound: 'designing the action in such a way that it is as interesting to the ear as to the eye';

5. character, object and décor: 'having characters interact with meaningful objects and with their physical setting';
6. simplicity and depth: 'keeping the story simple enough to be habitable by the viewer';
7. economy and wholeness: 'balancing the trimming away of all superfluous moments and detail so that the film is a concentrated distillation'.

(Raskin, 2002: 172)

EXERCISE
Analysing Your Story for the Seven Parameters

Using the outline for the story you completed in the previous exercise, examine it to identify the seven parameters listed by Raskin. Remember, a short film need not necessarily contain all seven, but identifying some of these elements in your own story should help you to see if you are developing an idea that is suitably focused for a short film.

	Raskin's seven parameters	Does your story contain this element? Yes/no	Give example(s) from your story
1	Character focus/character interaction		
2	Causality/choice		
3	Consistency/surprise		
4	Image/sound		
5	Character/object and décor		
6	Simplicity/depth		
7	Economy/wholeness		

FIGURE 5.2
Analysing your story for the seven parameters

Pitching Ideas

Contrary to what you might first believe, writing is not a solo process. It is important that you are able to communicate your ideas to other people vocally, and that these people understand your ideas. It is a way of testing out your potential audience or potential employer. If you do not test your ideas by sounding them out, how can you determine the way your audience will respond to your work?

Pitching in front of your tutors and peers is an invaluable exercise in script development. It is the first chance for you to find an audience, and the feedback process can be fun as well as productive when the comments are constructive. Pitching is also a confidence-builder and a useful employability skill.

EXERCISE
The Three-Minute Pitch for Fictional Works

Once you have an idea for your screenplay or for your short fictional film you should pitch it to an audience.

When pitching a script, it is best not to use visual aids because the words should speak for themselves. You should not read from the script, but can refer to prompt cards if you need to. Good eye contact is essential, as well as a large helping of enthusiasm!

Being succinct and precise is the key to a good pitch. You can refer to the previous exercise 'Structuring Your Project According to Todorov's Theory' to help structure your pitch.

You need to know your characters, the situation and the plot by heart, and be prepared for your audience to ask questions if there are any aspects of your script that they are unclear about.

- Before the pitch: Prepare the content and structure.
- During the pitch: Your audience should listen carefully to your ideas and, after you have finished speaking, they should be invited to give verbal comments and/or ask questions regarding your ideas.
- After the pitch: Make a note of the feedback you have received. You can refer to this when you make your next draft of the script.

Writing for Non-Fiction and Documentary

Stella Bruzzi points out that documentary is 'persistently treated as a representational mode of filmmaking' rather than simply a record of fact (Bruzzi, 2006: 11). Sheila Curran Bernard reiterates this. She says that 'factuality alone does not define documentary films; it's what the filmmaker does with those factual elements, artfully weaving them into an overall narrative that is often greater than the sum of its parts' (Curran Bernard, 2016: 2). In other words, non-fiction writing should still be considered as a form of 'storytelling'.

Bordwell and Thompson say that the labelling of documentary 'leads us to expect that the persons, places, and events shown to us exist' and that the information presented about them will be reliable (Bordwell and Thompson, 2017: 351). But if we consider for a moment the variety of ways that this information can be presented, then it highlights the idea that documentary is what we might call a 'constructed truth' and uses several narrative techniques to communicate its message.

Documentaries, like fictional works, still rely on character, situation and conflict to engage the viewer. They can be produced using a number of different techniques, such as filming in a 'fly-on-the-wall' style, using interviews or 'talking heads', or using a presenter. Whatever techniques you might choose to use, it is the underlying story and ability to compel the audience that should be at the forefront.

As well as documentaries, non-fiction forms also include corporate and instructional media that is produced for public consumption or for organisations to use in-house and includes training videos, material to recruit new members of staff and videos to advertise products or services. These non-fictional forms use a variety of storytelling techniques.

With works of fiction, creativity comes in the formation of ideas. Information videos, however, often use techniques such as animation and typography to consolidate the information. Another technique that may be used in non-fiction media is the voice-over. This can be an effective and economic way of condensing and communicating information – more so usually than written text, which can tend to overwhelm the viewer if there is too much information on screen. The exercise below will enable you to plan your non-fictional work in much the same way that you would plan a fictional piece.

EXERCISE
Creating a Plan for a Non-Fiction Form

First, consider the characters and situations that will be included. Second, think back to our analysis of narrative structure: equilibrium, disruption of equilibrium, recognition of disruption, attempt to repair disruption, reinstatement of initial equilibrium. Plan the narrative structure of your non-fiction piece. How is the theme introduced? Who are the main subjects? Where does it take place? What is the conflict? How is this resolved?

Consider the variety of ways the information will be presented. What techniques will you use (for example, filming in a fly-on-the-wall style, using interviews or talking heads, or using a presenter)?

How will you deal with information that is not easily filmed, such as statistics and lists of facts? Will you use voice-over, animation or typography?

Once you have constructed a detailed plan, you should have a good idea about the structure and form that your non-fictional work will take, and be able to discuss it with your brief provider, tutor and peers, or present it in a pitch.

Writing Interviews and Interview Questions for Audio-visual Media

In a previous chapter we discussed how to write questions for audience research questionnaires. We will now look at how to compose questions for onscreen interviews. Interviews can sometimes slow down action in audio-visual media, but can be useful if you want someone to recount a personal experience or if they have a vibrant or authoritative personality that will enhance your work.

In preparing for an interview, the person asking questions needs to show a genuine interest in what the interviewee has to say, or should have an understanding of the topic. An interviewer should prepare with some in-depth research, so that they can almost pre-empt what the interviewee will say. An interview conducted with a surface engagement by the interviewer will not elicit interesting answers from the interviewee, and the whole interview may appear flat and lifeless. Interview questions should be written carefully in order to draw satisfactory answers. You should try to avoid closed questions that will only gain short 'yes' and 'no' type answers. Take, for example, the following:

Q: What was your first job after leaving university?

A: I was a runner for an independent film.

A question structured in this way will probably elicit a short answer, and the interviewee will be waiting for a follow-up question. It does not make for a very satisfying answer because the question itself lacks depth.

However, a question framed in the following way requires the interviewee to give a longer answer, and makes for a much more satisfying response:

Q: Can you tell me a bit about your first job in the media after leaving university, how you got the job and what your duties were?

This is really three questions, condensed into one, and will help shape the answer into a form of narrative. For example, the interviewee will be taken back to their experience of leaving university, looking for work and going for an interview. They may have had several duties in this job, so this may also elicit several anecdotes. Before you know it, the interviewee will be doing all the talking! Your role then will be to keep the interviewee on topic, and also to possibly bring up further questions that you had not originally planned, but that may seem appropriate to the way the structure of the interview is going.

If possible, try not to include questions in the edited interview as these can slow the information down. Instead, write your questions in such a way that the answer will make it obvious what the question was. The answer to the latter question might start, for example, with the interviewee saying: 'When I first left university I saw a job advertised for a film runner ...' An answer like this does not require inclusion of the question in the final edit of the interview. You should also never incorporate onscreen questions in the form of written text. This is a lazy way of storytelling and disrupts the flow of the narrative.

If you are working on a production with a relatively short running time, then it is probably best not to rely too heavily on interviews if this does not suit the genre or form that you are using. If, however, your non-fiction text does use interviews to communicate most of its information, then it may be worth storyboarding your script to plan for sufficient cutaway or cover shots to help shape the video in post-production.

Eliciting satisfactory answers is even more important if you cannot use cutaways and cover shots. Imagine, for example, that you are producing an interview for radio. In this situation, the interviewer's questions must enable the interviewee to create pictures in the listener's head.

EXERCISE
Rewriting an Interview for Radio

You are producing a short radio interview about a recent graduate that has found employment in the media industry. Your aim is to find out about their work, how they found the job, and what background skills and experience they have brought to this job. This information is going to be used for undergraduates to listen to during a series of programmes on student radio during an 'employability day'.

Rewrite the following interview questions and/or restructure them. The presenter may make better use of some of the information, for example during an introduction, rather than as part of the interview. You should also consider ethics and tact in asking personal questions.

- What is your name?
- What do you do for a living?
- What was your first job?
- How did you get the job?
- What kind of things did you have to do in that job?
- Did you enjoy it?
- Are you still in the same job?
- If not, why did you leave?
- How much do you earn?
- What do you remember most about your time at university?
- Did you get good grades?
- What advice can you give the listeners about finding a good job in the media?

Pilot the above questions with one of your peers, to see what kind of answers you receive and whether you think they have enough depth. Then rephrase the questions to elicit in-depth answers that could be edited into an interview package. Once you feel that you have satisfactorily rewritten the interview questions, conduct them for real. You may even find some useful information and advice for when you graduate!

Storyboarding

Mark Simon suggests that there are many employment opportunities for storyboard artists including advertising agencies, live event designers, computer animation houses, theme park designers, and interactive and gaming companies (Simon, 2000: 26). It is good to see, therefore, that skills in storyboarding have a wide range of uses other than the film and television industries. A live event or a theme park ride takes us through a series of actions, images and tableaux, much like the narrative of a film or television programme. If you consider going into events management as a career, a storyboard might be a useful way of communicating your ideas to a client.

Creating a storyboard is a good test of your communication skills because the aim of a storyboard is to convey your ideas so that everyone on a crew can understand them. It enables others to visualise what the outcome will be.

FIGURE 5.3
Example of a storyboard

The storyboard will help you to plan all your shots before you go out on a shoot. Similarly, the storyboard will assist the editor, showing them how to sequence shots from the raw footage. You do not need to be an artist to produce a storyboard. If you are scared of drawing, then remember that it is much more scary to arrive at a video shoot with absolutely no plans down on paper about what shots you are going to choose, and how they will be used and sequenced in the finished video.

Nancy Beiman advises you start with thumbnail sketches first, referring to them as 'drawn thoughts', and suggests that you always 'work rough before going clean' (Beiman, 2007: 13). This is a useful tip for people who are nervous about drawing. Storyboard templates usually have a text box below each frame for you to fill in extra information, such as who is in the picture and what is happening.

EXERCISE
Storyboarding Using Post-it Notes

If you are nervous about drawing directly onto a storyboard template then you could try drawing your frames on post-it notes first. This gives you a sense of freedom and makes producing the storyboard less daunting. Carrying out this exercise emphasises the importance of being able to visualise your ideas. The aim here is to transfer the ideas in your head onto paper. Plan your storyboard by doing the following:

- Create a scenic breakdown (a list of each scene, and brief description of the action).
- Break each scene down into a list of potential images that make up that scene.
- Take a few post-it notes to start drawing on. Work in pencil first, before going over your images in pen. If you are not confident about drawing people, then you can simply represent them as 'stick people'.
- Lay your post-it notes out on a large sheet of paper. Rearrange them and add to them if necessary.
- Once you have finished using the post-it notes you can either stick them on to a storyboard template or redraw them, making them bold and more suitable for photocopying or scanning.
- Add extra information to the text boxes if you need to.
- Pilot your storyboard by showing it to your peers and make a note of their feedback.
- Is it detailed enough? Are there a sufficient number of images to represent the narrative you have in your head?

Once you are satisfied with the results you have your finished storyboard to aid production.

Tips and Hints about Storyboarding

- Use storyboarding to help you decide how to structure your narrative in a visual form.
- Use storyboards to visualise your ideas, enabling you to communicate your thoughts.

- Storyboarding can help save time when it comes to the shoot.
- Start with rough sketches then go neater.
- Use the text box below the image to add extra information.
- If you need to add or remove frames, cut your storyboards up and rearrange them.
- Produce images in high-contrast black and white for photocopying, scanning and sharing via email.
- A detailed storyboard will assist the production crew and editor.
- Never draw a storyboard to hand in as a piece of coursework *after* you have made your video. This is not only a *waste* of time (rather than a time saver) but it is always obvious!

Summary

This chapter has enabled you to kick-start your projects by thinking up ideas for fictional and non-fictional works. It has asked you to think about your work using analytical approaches to genre and narrative construction. It has given you tips and hints on how to structure your story-telling and given you guidance on how to pitch your ideas.

In the next chapter we will be looking at the design of settings, characters and props for your media project work.

Further Reading

For more information on narrative theory in film and documentary, the following references will be useful for you:

Bordwell, David, and Thompson, Kristin, 2017, *Film Art*, New York: McGraw-Hill.

Bruzzi, Stella, 2006, *New Documentary*, London: Routledge.

Curran Bernard, Sheila, 2016, *Documentary Storytelling*, Oxford: Focal Press.

Raskin, Richard, 2002, *The Art of the Short Fiction Film: A Shot by Shot Study of Nine Modern Classics*, London: McFarland & Company.

If you want to find out more about scriptwriting, these would be a good starting point:

Alessandra, Pilar, 2010, *The Coffee Break Screenwriter*, Studio City, CA: Michael Wiese Productions.

Ashton, Paul, 2011, *The Calling Card Script: A Writer's Toolbox for Stage, Screen and Radio*, London: A & C Black.

Musberger, Robert B., 2007, *An Introduction to Writing for Electronic Media: Scriptwriting Essentials Across the Genres*, Oxford: Focal Press.

Wells, Paul, 2007, *Scriptwriting*, Singapore: AVA Publishing.

To support your work on storyboarding you might want to look at:

Begleiter, Marcie, 2010, *From Word to Image: Storyboarding and the Filmmaking Process*, Studio City, CA: Michael Wiese.

Beiman, Nancy, 2007, *Prepare to Board! Creating Story and Characters for Animated Features and Shorts*, Oxford: Focal Press.

Simon, Mark, 2000, *Storyboards: Motion in Art*, Oxford: Focal Press.

6

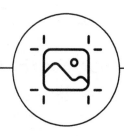

DESIGNING YOUR PROJECTS
Media Practice and Mise en Scène

After reading this chapter you will be able to:

- consider who and what should be included in your media texts;
- understand how cultural theory can inform the design of people, settings and props that are included in your practical work;
- understand how you might challenge the stereotypes that are often constructed in mainstream media.

Introduction

The previous chapter helped you to form ideas and to write scripts for your media projects. This chapter is about the design elements of your projects. In theoretical film studies these elements are referred to as mise en scène, which literally translates from French as 'putting into the scene'. Mise en scène can include settings, costumes, the position of characters within the frame, and how they interact with each other and the other elements in the picture. These are the elements that are covered in this chapter.

Mise en scène is most often used to describe and analyse an existing film text, but an understanding of mise en scène, and the way it constructs meaning, can also prove to be valuable to a media practitioner such as yourself when designing the content of your projects. This is appropriate to all types of visual media, such as still photography, advertising, animation and poster design.

The content elements we will examine include settings, costumes and people. The design of people or characters in your projects is particularly important because this can help to construct audience identification with the subject matter. The effect of the design elements on the audience should never be underestimated or taken for granted. When producing your texts, you can work actively to challenge dominant ideology by designing such elements with care and attention to detail. You need to think about who the audience will be and how they will engage with the characters and other elements of the mise en scène in your production.

The purpose of this chapter, then, is to enable you to consider who and what is included in your texts, and from what perspective they are represented.

Analysing the Mise en Scène

As a media-practice student, it is important to understand the codes and conventions on which audio-visual media are built. This is a skill you can improve and develop. You should be able to analyse your own work in the same way that you analyse media texts made by other people – for example mainstream media such as feature films, advertising and television programmes. It is helpful to expose the structured nature of such texts and examine some of its basic building blocks, so that you can use them in a meaningful way in your own projects.

The Construction and Representation of People

An analysis of the use of people in your media projects is a good starting point because much of media and cultural theory deals with representations and cultural identity. Most of the media texts you will produce include people. They are an important element in enabling your work to relate to its intended audience, so it is important that your design of people is carefully considered. This applies to fictional and non-fictional media.

It is important to remember that all people in media texts are designed, even those in non-fictional works such as a street interviewee. They are designed by being chosen from a range of possible participants by the producer and by the manipulation of the following: character type, costume, gesture, posture and proxemics. Each of these areas, or 'signs', can be interlinked in very important ways to denote and connote meaning, but we will examine each separately in the next few pages.

EXERCISE
Creating a Fictional Character Biography

It can help to create a biography or 'back story' for any character you are designing. The more background detail you can give your character, the more you will understand how they relate to the rest of the media text.

For the main characters in your media text, give a brief description of each of the following characteristics and then write a summary of how each characteristic has an effect on the design of the character:

Characteristic	Description	Effect on other elements of the media text/audience response
Age		
Gender		
Racial background		
Physical ability		
Physical appearance (height, build, colouring)		
Family status		
Main relationships		
How they relate to others		
Place of residence		
Type of housing		
Attitudes to life		
Political attitudes		
Interests and hobbies		
Educational background		
Employment status		
Social status (class)		
Main events in life so far		
Main hopes for rest of life		
Main fears for rest of life		
Other characteristics		

FIGURE 6.1
Character biography

You can see by filling in all the characteristics above that a detailed profile of a person has the potential to construct a fully formed, well-rounded character that your potential audience will relate to. The next step in constructing your character could be thinking about their personality traits, and how they interact with other people. It will enable you to realise how you would like your audience to understand the character and also the effect it will have on other characters within the text. The 'semantic differential' is a useful reference point here.

EXERCISE
The Semantic Differential

The 'semantic differential' scale was developed by Osgood, Suci and Tannenbaum in 1957 to gauge people's levels of social interaction and interpersonal communication (Knapp and Daly, 2011: 6). Use the semantic differential scale below to 'design' the main characters in your media projects.

In the column marked 'Character Trait' enter a variety of characteristics such as 'empathetic', 'fun-loving', 'aggressive', and so on.

In the rest of the grid put a tick or cross in the appropriate column (on a scale from 1 to 5) to identify how much or how little of these personality traits your character has.

You can apply this to all of the main characters in your media projects.

Character Trait	Semantic Differential				
	1 Very Little	2	3	4	5 Very much

FIGURE 6.2
The semantic differential

Stereotypes

Casting directors spend a lot of time looking for exactly the right person to play a part. However, the way that people are designed in media texts can sometimes result in the construction of stereotypes. Stereotyping is a process where visual shorthand is used to describe and represent people. It is the portrayal of people in an oversimplified and unquestioning way. As Barker points out, stereotyping 'commonly involves the attribution of negative traits to persons who are different to ourselves' (Barker, 2000: 208). Now read Barker's quote again carefully. It could be argued that this sentence in itself works ideologically to presume that we 'ourselves' are part of the dominant social order! This is why you should consider the construction of stereotypes with caution!

Stuart Hall argues that 'stereotyping tends to occur where there are gross inequalities of power. Power is usually directed against the subordinate or excluded group' (Hall et al., 2013: 248). These 'subordinate' or 'excluded' groups are usually contrasted with an imagined white, heterosexual, middle-class, male standard, 'against which inequalities are measured', but which itself is only one section of society (Pascale, 2013: xv). This results in negative stereotyping regarding race, sexuality, gender and class, for instance.

The Representation of Students in Mainstream Media

Rather than looking at racial, sexual, gender and class stereotypes, let us think for a moment about negative representations of students as a social subgroup, by considering the 'fly on the wall' documentary *The Secret Life of Students* (Channel 4, 2014). This is an example of a genre of documentaries that tend to air at the beginning of the academic year. Some of the critics of the programme tended to accept the representation of student life that the documentary constructed, whereas other reviewers commented that the participants were represented negatively as stereotypes. Michael Hogan in the *Telegraph* wrote:

> The popular perception of freshers is that they spend all their time playing drinking games, going on bar crawls, fiddling with their mobile phones and sleeping with each other. Depressingly, it turned out to be (almost) totally true. It's always pleasing when stereotypes get reinforced. (Hogan, 2014)

Beth Lambert in the *New Statesmen*, however, had this to say:

> These are not cutting-edge documentaries. These are production teams hunting down stereotypes and filming them in their natural habitat, cutting them together so as to reinforce as many stereotypes as possible … these programmes are part of the Jeremy Kyle school of thought, depicting predictable narratives which vilify groups which are already looked down upon by most of society. (Lambert, 2014)

Do you think that television programmes like this present an accurate portrayal of young adults? Do you find these programmes entertaining or do some of their negative representations aggravate you?

EXERCISE
Exercise on Preferred Readings of Characters

This exercise highlights how characters can be represented as stereotypes, and how you can challenge these stereotypes by constructing a preferred reading in the way that you design them. Following the four points below (character, stereotype, preferred reading and techniques to construct the preferred reading), design the following characters: a student, an elderly person, a homeless person, a Member of Parliament, a footballer's partner and a political activist.

Character	Stereotype	Preferred reading	Representational techniques
Student	Lazy, passive, unscholarly	Dedicated, assertive, studious	The character will be dressed smartly; will not look tired. They will be photographed working in the university library. Props such as a laptop and books will be used in the scene.
An elderly person			
A homeless person			
A Member of Parliament			
A footballer's partner			
A political activist			

FIGURE 6.3
Preferred readings of characters

You can see by completing the exercise above, and then adapting it for any character representation you want to include in your own media projects, that it is a useful way of avoiding the superficial representations of people that are often perpetuated by mainstream media.

The Use of Costume

Costume is an important point to consider in the construction of your media texts. Sarah Street asserts that it is important to 'recognise that film costumes not only relate to the characters who wear them but also to the audiences who watch them', and this is something to consider when dressing or designing the clothes for characters in your own media projects (Street, 2001: 7).

Costume designer Richard La Motte argues that 'Costumes become metaphors for your characters' character. The clothes reflect the times, action, station, conditions, and even inner turmoil of your screen characters, while the background costumes create the world that your main characters populate' (La Motte, 2010: 70). In other words, costumes help to construct authentic characters by projecting or communicating that person's characteristics for the audience to interpret. Landis also suggests that costumes play a part in a film's composition, '[providing] balance within the frame by using colour, texture, and silhouette' (Landis, 2012: 8). This can be applied to any media text in which people appear, and in which the costume constructs meaning as part of the general mise en scène along with settings, props and lighting, for example.

Costume includes hairstyle, make-up, clothes and jewellery, all of which are designed to communicate a particular message. These are considered even when people who are not fictional 'characters' are appearing in the text. You should consider what a costume is communicating by analysing what is worn, how it is worn, its condition, and its style and design. The costumes are a part of the narrative, whether this is a fictional or non-fictional piece of work.

Returning to the previous exercises you completed about creating a character biography, and their preferred reading, consider how the design of costume plays a part in character construction.

Tips for the design of costumes for your media-practice work:

- Design your costumes on paper first. Consider how they relate to the characters and story.
- Pay attention to detail. Think about how each element of the costume (clothes, hair dressing, make-up, accessories) contribute to the whole in terms of meaning.
- Make good use of available resources. You can create an impression of story and character with costume design, without having to be too literal.

Body Language and Proxemics

A useful way of connoting character is through the use of body language; namely the use of gesture, posture and proxemics (the use of personal space between people). Gesture can be used and manipulated to communicate the intended meaning of a media text, and is an important element for the audience to relate to. It includes facial expression, eye movement and the direction of a person or character's gaze.

When we communicate with another person we usually concentrate on the face and especially the eyes, and similarly members of an audience will usually 'read' a character's facial expression in order to understand how they should respond to the story. They will also follow a character's gaze in order to know where to look for important elements in an image. If a character's face is obscured from the audience's view it can create a sense of unease or mystery. Conversely, if a character is looking out of the image, at the viewer, we tend to focus on looking at them before looking at anything else.

Posture refers to the way people sit, stand and hold their body. It is closely related to gesture in the creation of an audience's understanding of a character. An image of a character standing rigid

FIGURE 6.4
The use of character's gaze to create meaning

FIGURE 6.5
The use of body posture

with their arms folded as illustrated in Figure 6.5 will communicate a different feeling to that of a character standing with a more welcoming pose.

Proxemics is derived from the word 'proximity' and refers to where people and characters stand in relation to each other, and in relation to the setting and props. For example, an image of a character seen in isolation will construct a different effect from an image of a character seen in relation to others. Similarly, an image of two characters standing or sitting close to each other or touching, will create a different effect from an image of two characters separated by a prop.

FIGURE 6.6
The use of proxemics

The Design of Settings

The place or surrounding that the narrative occurs in in a media text is referred to as the 'set' or 'setting'. It is important to consider how settings play a large part in constructing an audience's understanding of the text's meaning. Jane Barnwell reminds us that settings are 'not just a stage for the actors', but that they function as an 'interactive element of the narrative' and that 'the use of space and texture can create contrast and harmony that load the image with meaning' (Barnwell, 2004: 25). In a similar way to costumes, settings can reveal aspects about the characters' lives: 'their relative wealth, occupation, leisure pursuits, eating habits or favourite colour' or they may be used symbolically to reveal 'their inner life, desires and dreams' (Barnwell, 2004: 27).

The setting as a signpost for information about the life of the character onscreen can also apply to non-fictional work. Think carefully about where you place an interviewee. Are you interviewing them in a domestic space, or their place of work or leisure? What clues can be given by the setting about their attitudes and beliefs that will enable the viewer to understand more about the person on screen without them having to talk at length about themselves? Never place an interviewee against a blank wall – you will miss an opportunity to let the setting help tell a story!

Affron and Affron (1995: 37–39) theorise film settings in five levels of design intensity:

1. set as denotation (in which the set 'applies generic and cultural codes conventionally … and participates in narratives that claim minimal description');
2. set as punctuation (in which the set, released 'from its status as background [acquires] the potential to punctuate the narrative and thus make claims on the attention of the viewer');
3. set as embellishment (evidenced as 'spectacular sets' in 'colossal or spectacle films');
4. set as artifice (in which sets 'privilege their own artificiality');
5. set as narrative (in which the 'field of reading is composed of a single locale').

The two forms of settings that might be most applicable to student productions are the 'denotative' and the 'narrative'. For example, Affron and Affron say that sets whose function is 'essentially denotative carry a relatively small share of the narrative weight … [subscribing] to widely accepted depictions of the familiar, the everyday, the real as it corresponds to the spectator's direct experience of life' (Affron and Affron, 1995: 46). These types of settings are generally inconspicuous, and can help construct realism in a media text. They are undecorative and, importantly, can be 'designed' by utilising what is at hand. This could be a short film shot on campus or in your halls of residence, for example.

Affron and Affron's taxonomy of 'set as narrative' is a useful way of analysing short-form, low-budget, student productions (such as music videos, viral animations and vlogs) 'whose narratives propose a generally circumscribed spatial field and whose art direction disposes its actual limits' (Affron and Affron, 1995: 158). In other words, the supposed limitations of a single setting can in actual fact be considered as a positive feature, and a significant part of the storytelling. Imagine, for example, a narrative constructed entirely within the confines of a lift! … or a film shot in an alley way … or a story about two people meeting on a bus journey.

Production designer Ken Adam argues that 'the point of production design is to create an idea of a place' rather than to recreate 'reality' in an architectural sense (Frayling, 2005: 80). You should keep this in mind when working on a tight budget. Just a few simple props, a carefully chosen location or even a carefully selected portion of a location can construct an impression of a place, without having to faithfully re-create it.

Tips for the design of settings for your media-practice work:

- Design your setting on paper first and relate it to the story you are telling.
- Let the setting 'speak' to your audience, and let it help to communicate your intended meaning.
- Think about how each part of the setting contributes to the whole in terms of meaning (for example the walls, the floors, window dressings, the fixtures and the fittings).

The Use of Props

The next element to examine in mise en scène is the use of props (short for 'properties'). Props are important elements in the construction of meaning, whether you are creating a factual or fictional media text. There are three main types of props in media production:

1. Dressing props: decorative features on the set such as a vase of flowers.
2. Action props: any object used to advance the narrative such as a phone being answered.
3. Personal props: anything used or worn by the characters or performers that helps to construct meaning, but is not integral to the development of the story, such as a rucksack on someone's back.

Dressing props are more closely associated with the settings, but are important in helping to construct atmosphere, and give clues to the audience about how characters relate to the environment in which the text is set. Action props are more closely related to the construction of narrative, whilst personal props might help the audience to understand more about the nature of the characters.

Commutation

Roland Barthes' *commutation test* demonstrates how settings, props and characters construct meaning in media texts. Changes are introduced to the signifiers – in this case, the settings, props and characters – to observe how this alters the overall meaning of the text. For example, what would be the effect of the following alterations to the photo in Figure 6.7?

- What if this were set in a city street at night?
- What if it were set outside an upmarket hotel?
- What if the character on the left were a woman in her nineties?
- What if the empty space on the left of the bench was occupied by a police officer?
- What if the character on the left was wearing an elaborate ball gown?
- What if the leather shoulder bag in the centre of the two characters were changed for a rolled-up sleeping bag?
- What if the shoulder bag were changed for a briefcase?

FIGURE 6.7
Commutation test original image

After reflecting on the above, have a go at producing your own illustrations of commutation.

EXERCISE
Costume, Settings and Props Commutation

Find a digital image that includes character/s, costume/s, setting and prop/s (either fiction or non-fiction). What is the intended meaning of the image you have chosen? Using an image manipulation program, take turns to change, remove or add one or more of the following elements:

- Character/s
- Costume/s
- Setting
- Prop/s

Consider the effect this change has made on the meaning of the text, and how it has altered your understanding of the story. Reflect on the importance of settings, costumes and props and how these help to inform meaning in your own media projects.

Summary

By reading this chapter, and completing the practical exercises included, you have learned about the importance of mise en scène in helping to construct meaning and give substance to your scripts and ideas. You have learned to think about the significance of settings, props and people, and how these elements should not be taken for granted. You have learned that dominant ideological representations do not occur by 'accident', and that lazy, engrained media representations should and can be confronted and challenged.

In the next chapter we will look at the technical elements of audio-visual production such as lighting, colour, composition and camerawork. These will enhance your storytelling techniques.

Further Reading

The following book will help to deepen your understanding of media and cultural representations of people:

Hall, Stuart, Evans, Jessica, and Nixon, Sean, 2013, *Representation*, London: Sage.

These books will be useful for finding out more about costume design in film and television:

Landis, Deborah Nadoolman, 2012, *Costume Design*, Oxford: Focal Press.

La Motte, Richard, 2010, *Costume Design 101: The Business and Art of Creating Costumes for Film and Television*, Studio City, CA: Michael Wiese.

Street, Sarah, 2001, *Costume and Cinema: Dress Codes in Popular Film*, London: Wallflower.

For more guidance on production design, the following are worth a read:

Affron, Charles, and Affron, Mirella Jona, 1995, *Sets in Motion*, New Brunswick, NJ: Rutgers University Press.

Barnwell, Jane, 2004, *Production Design: Architects of the Screen*, London: Wallflower.

Frayling, Christopher, 2005, *Ken Adam, and the Art of Production Design*, London: Faber and Faber.

To look further into Barthes' commutation test, see the following:

Chandler, Daniel, 2007, *Semiotics: The Basics*, London: Routledge (pages 88–90).

7

CONSTRUCTING YOUR PROJECTS
The Technical Elements of Media Practice

After reading this chapter you will be able to:

- consider how lighting can be used effectively to enhance your media projects;
- understand how effective design of a colour scheme can construct meaning;
- examine how to frame and compose images for effective communication;
- determine how camera and subject movement can enrich your storytelling, and construct the illusion of a three-dimensional space.

Introduction

In the previous chapter we examined how mise en scène (settings, props and people) can be manipulated to enhance meaning and contribute to the narrative of your projects. You should now consider some of the techniques you can use to *treat* the mise en scène in order to enhance communication. Design of lighting, design of a colour scheme, composition and camera work are the focus of this chapter.

The Use of Lighting

You will always be working with two types of light – natural or artificial light. You should decide which is most appropriate for the scene you are creating. Natural light (light from the sun) will have different levels of intensity and therefore different connotations of mood due to weather conditions and the time of the day. The use of additional, artificial lighting (electric lighting) will give you more control over a scene.

You should always remember that light is not simply used to illuminate the scene we are being shown, but to construct and enhance a message. The use of shadow is equally important. As Bordwell and Thompson argue:

> Lighter and darker areas within the frame help create the overall composition of each shot and thus guide our attention to certain objects and actions. A brightly illuminated patch may draw our eye to a key gesture, while a shadow may conceal a detail or build up suspense about what may be present. (Bordwell and Thompson, 2017: 125)

In order to fully control lighting in any visual medium, be it photography, film or video, you should try not to mix natural light and electric light. If you are photographing or filming indoors, then it is best to use artificial light in order to manipulate the light source to enhance communication of the intended reading. There are three main ways to manipulate the light sources that you use:

- Intensity – the manipulation of the brightness that can be increased or reduced for different effects.
- Direction – the pointing of the light source to draw attention to particular areas of the image, or to create shadows.
- Filters – the softening of shadows using gels or their use to create patterns in the light.

By using these techniques, you are using light as a 'pointing stick', leading the viewer's eye to the meaning within a picture. This is similar to some of the techniques discussed earlier with a character's posture and gesture.

One of the most commonly referred-to lighting set-ups is that of three-point lighting. Three-point lighting uses:

- a key light to illuminate the most important element of a shot or scene;
- a fill light to soften the area of shadow cast by the key light;
- a back light, to separate the foreground from the background.

The effect of such a lighting set-up is not only to draw attention to the most important element of the image (for example an interviewee), but also to create a sense of three-dimensional space.

In some instances – especially if you have limited resources, limited time to set up lights, or if you are filming in a small space – it may be possible to light a scene using one light as a key light, and a reflector to softly brighten the areas that are in shadow. Reflectors are also useful for this purpose when filming outdoors in natural light.

The best way to learn how to light different scenes is through trial and practice. You should always ensure that you light a scene creatively and to the best advantage of the story you are trying to convey. The following exercise will help you to practise ways of creating or enhancing meaning with light.

EXERCISE
Manipulation of Light

Before experimenting with electric lighting in a three-dimensional space, you might want to try manipulating light with photographic images that you have found online, or that you already have on your phone.

Choose a small selection of images and upload them into some image-manipulation software. Manipulate the light in the images to draw attention to important parts of the picture, and to conceal specific areas of the image. Experiment by:

- altering the brightness;
- altering the contrast;
- masking areas of the image in darkness;
- highlighting areas of the image in light.

Think about the effect that these have had on the meaning of the images and how you could use similar techniques in your own work.

Tips for Using Light in Your Projects

- If filming or photographing outdoors in bright sunlight try to avoid having the light source behind your subject – it will turn your subject into a silhouette.
- Similarly, when photographing someone indoors avoid positioning them with a window behind. This too, will turn your subject into a silhouette.
- Try to avoid positioning a person so that they are facing the sun, as this will probably make them squint.
- If photographing or filming indoors, try not to mix natural and electric light.
- Use electric light to control and manipulate the light in a scene to your desired effect.
- Light a subject so that they are positioned away from a background (such as a wall) to eliminate unwanted shadows.
- Remember that shade is just as important as light for creating space, depth and texture.
- If working with limited light resources, use a reflector to light the subject. A reflector can be made simply out of a sheet of white card or similar.

Designing a Colour Scheme

In a similar way that you can manipulate light, you can control and design the use of colour in your media projects. You should 'design' the colour elements of an image carefully by selecting the colours that will appear in the frame, and eliminating colours that disrupt or detract from the mood that you are aiming for. You should think carefully about how an audience will 'read' and interpret the colours in an image that you have created.

Warm colours such as red and orange tend to stand out from an image, whereas cold colours such as blue and green will recede into the background. For example, a character wearing bright red in a room full of other people wearing cool colours or pastel shades will dominate the scene and catch the viewer's eye. In other words, colours such as red can be used as a 'pointing stick' to highlight important areas of an image, and guide the viewer's attention to crucial elements of the story or message.

As well as using colour to enhance composition, create depth and highlight important areas of an image, you should also consider how an audience might respond emotionally or culturally to the colours you use. Patti Bellantoni (2012) highlights the storytelling functions of colour. For example, she describes reds as powerful, lusty, defiant, angry or romantic; yellows as exuberant, or innocent and idyllic; blues as cerebral, melancholy or passive; and greens as healthy and vital, or poisonous and corrupt.

One of the ways you can work with colour for your projects is by thinking about it at the planning or storyboard stage. Think about creating an overall 'colour palette'. For example, you might want to deliberately avoid using strong, bright colours if you wish to create a muted or sombre mood. If you make notes on a storyboard about the colour palette of a scene, you can make sure that the settings, props and costumes adhere to this too, and you can inform the people who appear in your texts to avoid wearing certain colours when they are filmed or photographed.

EXERCISE
Manipulating Colour

Download a small selection of images from the internet or take some photographs with your phone. These could be portraits, landscapes and photographs of food, for example. Try and select images that largely depend on their use of colour to communicate a certain response. Upload the photographs into some image-manipulation software. Experiment with the use of colour by manipulating it in the following ways:

- Increase the saturation.
- Decrease the saturation.
- Alter a colour picture into black and white.
- Isolate one object in the picture that you want to keep in colour. Now drain the rest of the image of its colour, so that it has a low saturation or is in black and white.
- Manipulate an image so that easily identifiable objects (such as food) have an entirely new colour.

Consider the following questions about the effect of manipulating the colour in the images:

- How has it altered your reading of the images?
- How does it change the mood or alter your emotional response?
- How has it emphasised certain parts of the image, and detracted from others?
- Has it made the image more aesthetically pleasing or less so?

Tips for Using Colour in Your Media Projects

- Always design colour schemes for your projects at the pre-production and planning stage. Remember it is easier to design colour in pre-production than it is to alter it in post-production.
- Use complementary colours to create harmony in an image.
- Use contrasting colours to create spatial depth.
- If a 'warm' object appears in shot that detracts from the main object of interest, then move it out of shot.
- Think about the emotional impact and cultural significance of colours.

The Use of Visual Effects

Visual effects refer to the alteration of the original image using effects. There are two types of visual effects: natural effects and artificial visual effects.

A natural visual effect might be the addition of wind, smoke, steam, reflections, and so on to an image or scene when it is photographed, whereas an artificial visual effect is created through the use of the camera, or more often in post-production. Artificial visual effects can include colour tints or filters, shaped filters, focus (hard or soft), superimposition, soft or grainy textures, coloration and masking. Adding shaped filters to an image – for example to imply that the image is seen through binoculars, a keyhole or a gun site – can suggest voyeurism, or make the subject appear vulnerable.

Although visual effects can be created using image-manipulation software, Pramaggiore and Wallis point out that 'practitioners in the field are constantly developing and perfecting new effects ... so any discussion of techniques becomes out of date very quickly' (Pramaggiore and Wallis, 2008: 173). With this in mind, it is more important to consider the meanings that are constructed by visual effects, rather than discuss the production processes of the techniques themselves. As with other technical elements, the skill is to apply visual effects that enhance rather than detract from the main message or meaning of the image or story.

The most important consideration when planning the use of visual effects is that they are not just there to 'pretty up' the picture. They should first and foremost be used to enhance communication. If used wisely visual effects can direct the audience to the preferred reading of an image. If used inappropriately they can very easily disrupt the intention of the piece.

The following exercise will help you to practise using visual effects to enhance meaning in your work.

EXERCISE
Using Visual Effects to Manipulate the Meaning of an Image

You will most probably have numerous picture-related apps on your phone, and therefore will be familiar with the way that manipulating colour, lighting, focus and filters can alter a photograph. Why not try using these effects as part of your project work?

Take a photograph or small selection of photographs of different subjects on your phone; for example, portraits, photographs of your dinner, a picture of a landscape and a picture of some architecture.

Now manipulate each photograph in the following ways:

- Alter the texture of the image using a variety of filters, such as making it more grainy or more painterly.
- Alter the areas of focus so that some areas appear more sharply in focus than others.
- Add different style frames to your pictures, such as a circular shape, a love heart, a vignette, a gilt frame or torn paper.

Experiment with some of these techniques to construct different emotional and cultural meanings using these keywords:

> lifeless;
>
> modernity;
>
> nostalgia;
>
> warmth;
>
> hilarity;
>
> depression;
>
> ominous;
>
> vivid.

Now analyse *why* you think you responded to the images in these ways as a result of your manipulation of visual effects. Reflect on how you might also use some of these techniques in your own project work.

Tips for Using Visual Effects in Your Projects

- Plan your use of visual effects during pre-production via the storyboard.
- Use visual effects to enhance the intended meaning, rather than detract from it.
- Avoid overuse of visual effects or they will lose their impact.

Framing the Image

In their book *Grammar of the Shot*, Christopher Bowen and Roy Thompson discuss several different elements that should be considered in each individual shot of audio-visual production. Some of these elements refer to aesthetic and compositional elements, but importantly Bowen and Thompson emphasise that each shot should also include *motivation* and *information* that carry the story forward and enhances the meaning for its audience (Bowen and Thompson, 2009: 28–33). For example, a shot can help to tell the audience information such as:

- who the media text is about;
- where they are;
- what they are doing.

The framing of an image is largely taken for granted by audiences. Framing works ideologically to construct and *naturalise* an audience's reading of a text. It is only when the framing of an image is poor, or does not follow an audience's expectations, that framing draws attention to itself – think, for example, of poorly photographed holiday snaps where a person's head is cropped out of the frame!

Framing helps to tell the viewer where to look, because the person who frames the picture makes an informed decision about what to include and what to exclude from the frame. As Pramaggiore and Wallis explain, 'Camera placement may evoke a wide range of emotions: the position of the camera may compel intimacy or establish a sense of distance from characters and situations. It is also important to remember what the camera placement excludes' (Pramaggiore and Wallis, 2008: 139).

Shot Sizes

The following standard shot sizes and their abbreviations may be familiar to you from film studies modules, as well as media-practice modules. It is worth repeating this here to consider the context in which each shot type might be used in your project work.

> **Establishing shot (ES)**, sometimes referred to as extreme long shot (ELS) – usually a shot of a location such as a landscape or building. A human figure will not be the main subject of a shot this wide because they may be too small to see.

FIGURE 7.1
Establishing shot (ES)

Very long shot (VLS) – this will usually show a figure and their surroundings.

FIGURE 7.2
Very long shot (VLS)

Long shot (LS) – a shot of your subject (a person) from head to toe. Or a shot of more than one person. For example, a 'two-shot' – two people – from head to toe.

FIGURE 7.3
Long shot (LS) seen here as a two-shot

Medium shot or mid shot (MS) – this will include more detail. For example, a medium shot or mid shot will frame a person from the waist up handling a prop.

FIGURE 7.4
Medium shot (MS)

Close-up (CU) – a close-up will frame a person's head and shoulders. This shot size is useful for interviews, or for images of a person where you might want to show facial expressions and emotion, but still convey a sense of space.

FIGURE 7.5
Close-up (CU)

Big close-up (BCU) – this frames the full face of a person and is used for dramatic effect or to show details such as which direction your subject is looking towards. This is best framed by cropping the top of the head rather than the person's chin.

FIGURE 7.6
Big close-up (BCU)

Extreme close-up (ECU) – this is used to show specific details as in the example below.

FIGURE 7.7
Extreme close-up (ECU)

There are some other things to consider when framing shots. For example, are you framing the subject from a high angle or low angle, or with a camera at their eye level?

- Eye level tends to look natural and is therefore neutral in its construction of meaning, and the way the subject relates to the viewer.

- A camera positioned from a high or low angle can be used to create a dramatic effect.

FIGURE 7.8
Use of low angle and high angle

You should also frame your subjects so that they have enough space for *looking* and *moving* into the frame. In terms of space for looking, your subject should look 'into' the frame not out of the edge of the frame. This is known as 'looking room' or 'nose room'. Your shot should anticipate which direction your subject is going to move towards. This is similar in principle to 'looking room', but is sometimes referred to as 'walking room'. The same concept applies whether the subject is walking, running, driving or cycling. The use of 'looking room' and 'walking room' also relates to composition, because the framing of people and characters in this way helps to create stability in an image.

FIGURE 7.9
Creating looking room with composition where the subject is looking into the empty space in the frame

FIGURE 7.10
Poor composition where the subject has no space in the frame to look into

FIGURE 7.11
Creating walking room with composition where the subject is walking into the empty space in the frame

FIGURE 7.12
Poor composition where the subject has no space in the frame to walk into

An exercise at the end of this chapter will give you opportunity to practise using a range of different types of shots, but first we consider the importance of composition.

The Use of Composition

As well as lighting, colour, visual effects and shot types, you should think about the use of composition in your project work. A fundamental of composition is symmetry. This is one way of creating balance in an image. However, it is rare that the main point of interest in an image is always placed at the centre of the frame. It can appear more aesthetically pleasing to place the main subject of an image off-centre, either to the right or left of the frame, for example using 'looking room' as described above.

The use of perspective can be considered as a 'depth cue'. It helps to construct an impression of three-dimensionality and space in a two-dimensional image. The way that parallel horizontal lines recede into the distance and converge is referred to as a 'vanishing point'. Placing the main subject of an image – such as a person – in the foreground of a vanishing point can create perspective, and therefore depth. It can also be used to guide the viewer to look at an important part of the image.

You can also arrange points of interest in the foreground and background of an image, in order to construct a sense of depth and visual interest in much the same way that creating lines of perspective with vanishing points does in your compositions.

FIGURE 7.13
Example of perspective where the line of the path and the bench slats creates a depth cue

The Moving Elements

As we have found from the above, composition and framing can help to determine what the dominant elements of the image are. The difference with a moving image, however, is that composition and framing should be carefully considered in each successive shot. The timing of each image or shot also needs to be considered in order for the audience to 'read' the image.

Bordwell and Thompson highlight that it is 'mobile framing' – camera movement – that differentiates the framing of film and video from other visual media such as paintings, photographs and comic strips (Bordwell and Thompson, 2017: 194).

In moving-image production it is important to consider both the subject movement and the camera movement, and also how these relate to each other. For example, if the subject/s within the frame (a person or persons) are moving, the camera might follow them to keep them in shot, or it may keep still and allow the subject/s to create new compositions within the frame, or even exit the frame.

Pramaggiore and Wallis suggest that a 'camera that remains in the same position may produce a sense of stagnation', whereas a 'moving camera may encourage viewers to become involved in a character's physical or psychological sensations' (Pramaggiore and Wallis, 2008: 146). All of these considerations are dictated by the narrative, or story content, whether fiction or non-fiction. An illusion of depth and space can also be constructed when a camera tracks around a subject, or when pans and tilts help to define a continuity of space between subjects.

In other words, camera movement – along with subject movement and perspective – works to deceive the audience that they are watching a three-dimensional space, rather than the flat plane of the cinema screen, television screen, computer monitor or mobile phone.

The names of the following camera movements are part of a common language in moving-image production and audio-visual design, but some of the terms are often confused with others, and therefore it may be useful to go through them here:

- The pan (derived from 'panorama'): a horizontal camera move, either from left to right, or from right to left (for example a camera shot that moves across a wide landscape that could not be captured satisfactorily in a single, motionless shot).

- The tilt: a vertical camera move, either upward or downward (for example a camera shot that moves upwards as it traces a tall building from the ground to the top).

- The cant: a diagonal camera move. This can be constructed in four different ways: from bottom left of the frame to top right, from bottom right of the frame to top left, from top left of the frame to bottom right, or from top right of the frame to bottom left. It is difficult to achieve a satisfactory cant without professional equipment – such as a camera crane – although you could try it with a handheld camera.

- Tracking: a shot in which the camera follows the moving subject, usually with the aid of tracks (hence the name) or a camera 'dolly'. The resultant shot gives the impression of an ever-changing, moving background and foreground, whilst the main subject remains in shot.

- The zoom: a shot in which the camera stays fixed, but the zoom facility is used to either magnify (zoom in) or de-magnify (zoom out) a point of interest in the shot. The zoom-in can be used to move in and highlight a detail that you want the audience to see, and the zoom-out can help to reveal more information about the space around a subject or detail.

Tips for Using Camera Movement in Your Video Projects

- Camera movements should be planned ahead, preferably at the storyboard stage.
- Use camera movements appropriately to enhance the story rather than detract from it.
- Start and end each camera movement with a composed shot.
- Camera movements are often best performed with the aid of a tripod, but this largely depends on the style and mood of the media text you are producing.
- Consider using a handheld camera to produce a particular effect, such as a *cinema verité* style, or the idea of someone being followed.

The following exercise should help you consolidate all that we have covered in this chapter about the technical elements of audio-visual communication. It is based on *Exercise Movie* (1958), three films produced following the same basic outline, each with a different approach. The full story is discussed in Shand and Craven's book *Small-Gauge Storytelling, Discovering the Amateur Fiction Film* (2013).

The three short *Exercise Movie* films were produced for the magazine *Amateur Cine World* by a beginner new to film-making, an experienced amateur and a professional film-maker.

The experiment was conducted because many readers' letters to *Amateur Cine World* often asked if they should buy the latest model of cine camera in order to produce the best-quality films. The authors of the magazine who devised the experiment wanted to prove that it was the planning and the thought behind the filming that mattered most. You can find out more about *Exercise Movie* on the Scotland on Screen archive website (scotlandonscreen.org.uk).

EXERCISE
Re-creating *Exercise Movie*

Create a storyboard based on the scenario below:

> A woman walks up to a bench and sits beside a man. The woman is eating sandwiches and feeding pigeons. The man falls asleep beside her and leans over her handbag, trapping it. The woman blows up a paper bag and bangs it, waking the man up and freeing her bag. She takes her bag and runs off.

The instructions on the storyboard should be to a level of detail where it could be handed to somebody else for them to film.

Think carefully about how to observe the conventions of lighting, colour, visual effects and composition. Aim to include at least one of each of the following shot types and camera movements on the storyboard:

- establishing shot (ES);
- very long shot (VLS);
- long shot (LS);

- medium shot or mid shot (MS);
- medium close-up (MCU);
- big close-up (BCU);
- extreme close-Up (ECU);
- angle below;
- angle above;
- looking room;
- walking room;
- zoom;
- pan;
- tilt;
- cant;
- handheld;
- tracking shot.

You could follow this up by making the film or by handing your storyboard to someone else to film. It might also be interesting to compare your own version with others' and how the results reflect the level of planning undertaken.

Summary

By reading this chapter, and completing the practical exercises included here, you have learned how light, colour and visual effects help to emphasise the most important visual elements in the frame. You have considered how composition and framing help to draw attention to the important elements of a scene. You have also examined how camera movement and subject movement can help to construct the illusion of a three-dimensional space.

You are now ready for the production stage of your projects, which is discussed in the following chapter.

Further Reading

To explore lighting and cinematography further, several chapters from these books would be useful:

> Bordwell, David, and Thompson, Kristin, 2017, *Film Art*, New York: McGraw-Hill.
> Pramaggiore, Maria, and Wallace, Tom, 2011, *Film: A Critical Introduction*, London: Laurence King Publishing.

Further instruction on lighting and shot types for your productions can be found in the following books:

Lyver, Des, and Swainson, Graham, 2005, *Basics of Video Lighting*, Oxford: Focal Press.

Millerson, Gerald, 2006, *Lighting for Video*, Oxford: Focal Press.

Bowen, Christopher, and Thompson, Roy, 2009, *Grammar of the Shot*, Oxford: Focal Press.

The following book explains colour theory and its application in more depth:

Bellantoni, Patti, 2012, *If It's Purple, Someone's Gonna Die: The Power of Color in Visual Storytelling*, Oxford: Focal Press.

8

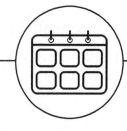

ORGANISING MEDIA PRODUCTION
Production Roles and Administration

After reading this chapter you will be able to:

- organise and plan your video projects;
- recognise different production roles and duties;
- understand the importance of production administration and ethics including health and safety, and copyright laws.

Introduction

This chapter focuses on the production stage of video projects, and in particular how the preparation you have made in building your team can be put into practice. The information and exercises based on team building and team dynamics in Chapter 2 will have prepared you for the production stage of your projects, which is outlined here.

First, we will look at some of the key production roles in media practice. Then we will highlight the importance of administration and organisation. Effective communication and planning in media production are skills that can be transferred to a range of employment contexts where your work is dependent on bringing groups of people together and organising the effective use of time. This includes events management, video production or arranging a photo shoot for a magazine or website.

One of the best ways to maximise efficiency and effectiveness during your production is to ensure that everyone in the team is working to a shared purpose, knows what the aims of the production are, and also that they are aware of everyone's duties.

Administration and paperwork – usually collated in a production log or production diary – is the best way to ensure that the team is fully aware of all the jobs that have already been done, the jobs that need to be done, and who is responsible for performing these duties. We will be referring to some useful production documents later on in the chapter to guide you through these points.

Production work is never easy, but the satisfaction of completing some very hard work and overcoming problems is very rewarding, and can enhance your employability skills, no matter what career you choose to go into.

Production Teams

The scale and type of your production team may vary according to your project brief or the type of assessment. You might be working on a large-scale production in which a large number of students from your course or module are working in specific roles throughout the project's duration. On the other hand, you could be working on a smaller-scale assignment in teams of about four, where you each have 'floating' roles throughout the project. A small documentary crew involved in interviewing delegates at a conference, or shooting 'vox-pops' in the street, might only consist of three people: the camera person, the sound recordist and the interviewer. These roles might be doubled up with producer, director and editor, for example.

If you are in a small team and changing duties throughout the project, then you should aim to ensure that everyone knows what their duty is on a specific day or at a specific location. This will prevent any potential problems arising from a situation where you think that a duty has been covered by one of the other members of the team, and they make the mistake of thinking you are responsible.

We will now look in further detail at production roles specific to video projects, and the responsibilities of each role.

The Producer

Your producer is responsible for overseeing the whole project. They will work closely with your director and screenwriter in bringing the project to life, making contact and communicating with all the members of the team, liaising with project-brief providers, scheduling and sending out call sheets. The producer also has to ensure that the team observes health and safety regulations. A summary of the producer's tasks includes:

- gathering the crew together and helping to assign production roles;
- communicating with project clients;
- recruiting people to appear on camera (actors/interviewees);
- scheduling the production (dates and times);
- liaising with local businesses and property owners to find locations.

Your producer has a lot of responsibility, needs to be very well organised, efficient and have excellent communication and leadership skills. This person is effectively your production team leader.

The Production Assistant

Your production assistant is responsible for much of a project's administration. They look after call sheets, scripts, consent forms, and so on. They might also perform other duties such as logging shots during a video shoot. A good production assistant needs to be highly organised, good at administrating and distributing essential paperwork, and also be very good at communicating with the director, and the rest of the team. Their production tasks include:

- sending out call sheets;
- asking people to sign consent forms before being filmed;
- filling out health and safety forms;
- logging shots during the shoot;
- collating all your administration documents in a production log.

The Director

Your director manages the technical crew and brings a performance out of the actors, presenters or interviewees during the shoot. The director needs to be assertive without being bossy, and to keep his or her mind – and the minds of the crew – focused on the aims of the project. The director must be able to work under pressure and be able to adapt to unpredictable situations. They should also be able to instil confidence in the rest of your team.

Camera Operator

Your camera operator is responsible for capturing all the important action of a scene in the most appropriate way for communicating the 'story' to the audience, and this applies to both fiction and non-fiction. The camera operator works closely with your director and makes all the decisions about setting up the camera, and lighting the image. This person also refers to the storyboard in order to see what size each shot needs to be, what will be included in the frame, and if any camera movements are involved.

Your camera operator is also responsible for making sure batteries are charged, and that the camera and other relevant pieces of kit such as the tripod are in working order. Dead batteries and an unsteady tripod have ruined numerous shoots in the past, simply because the camera operator did not check the kit before leaving for the location.

Clapperboard Operator

The use of clapperboards originates from traditional film productions where the audio track was recorded on a separate format (for example tape) to the image track (the film). However, the use of clapperboards is also useful for digital productions. Clapperboards not only identify the scene and take numbers at the beginning of each shot, but the 'clap' sound that it makes can help you to synch up the audio and visual tracks if you choose to record audio on a separate device from the visuals, or if you choose to separate the audio and visuals on the timeline of your project whilst editing.

Even with digital video that enables you to delete unwanted clips during or after filming, and to name clips once you upload them to the software, it is good practice to use a clapperboard on set as part of a 'record routine' and to facilitate teamwork.

Sound Recordist

In a small crew the two roles of sound recordist and boom operator will probably be conflated. Your boom operator's job is to position the microphone as close to the sound source as possible and to make sure that information that is important to the 'story' is recorded competently. The recordist needs to listen out for any noise interferences that can be detected through the microphone, but that might not be immediately obvious to other people on set. Sound recording must be monitored through headphones to ensure its quality.

The sound recordist needs to be very observant with both ear and eye, anticipating or thinking ahead to where the next important sound is coming from. They also have to be patient because the boom operator often has to stand for long periods of time holding the boom pole!

The Lighting Director

Your lighting director is responsible for designing the most appropriate lighting for a particular scene. This includes working with the director and camera operator to find the best place to stand outdoors when setting up a shot; for example, noticing the direction of light from the sun, whether the subject is in or out of shadows, whether reflectors need to be used, and so on. The lighting director may also work closely with the production/set designer if the aesthetic qualities of the scene are dependent on how the settings are lit. When using artificial lighting, your lighting director will not only illuminate the set so that the action can be seen, but will also observe how the use of both light and shade will construct the illusion of a three-dimensional image in the finished media text.

The person responsible for the lighting needs to look into the viewfinder to determine how best to position and adjust the intensity of the lights. On a small crew, it may be that your camera operator is also responsible for the lighting, and in this case it is a good idea for them to keep checking the lighting through the viewfinder, while the lights are being set up.

The Design Team (Settings, Props, Costume)

Depending on the size of your production, the roles of set-dressing, prop design, costume and make-up may be overseen by one or several people headed by the production designer. Designing an overall 'look' and 'feel' to a production can aid continuity between shots and scenes. Another important dimension to production design is its ability to construct meaning to character and plot by enhancing the mise en scène.

Whilst on set, the design team should keep an eye on the storyboard and plans for the production and work accordingly. This will involve:

- dressing the set;
- gathering props and making them available at appropriate points;
- overseeing the costume: on some of your productions, actors, presenters and interviewees might wear their own clothes and make-up – however, some prior discussion with the design team about the appropriate 'look' of these elements is still very important.

The Continuity Supervisor

The role of the continuity supervisor can often be overlooked in student productions. However, this role can be crucial if you are shooting a story out of sequence on a single camera. When we look at 'classical continuity editing' in the next chapter, you will understand how vital continuity is in constructing the illusion of continuous action in a sequence, even if this occurs across several 'cuts'. This includes continuity of action and movement across different shots in the same sequence but also, importantly, continuity in the mise en scène (costume, hair, handling of props, and so on).

Your continuity supervisor must have a very keen eye and ear, and a lot of patience. They may have to watch a scene being recorded over and over again, and keep an eye on all the nuances of speech and movement in every take. If you are easily distracted and feel the need to check your phone every five minutes, then this role is probably not for you!

The following exercise will demonstrate the responsibility of the continuity supervisor, and also help your crew to plan the best way to organise the scheduling and filming of scenes.

EXERCISE
Reordering Your Narrative to Suit Continuity

Make a photocopy of your storyboard. Cut out all the frames so that they are like a pack of cards. Plan the order that the shots are best to be filmed in. Rearrange all the storyboard frames to follow a shooting schedule, rather than the narrative sequence.

For example:

a.   Rearrange all outdoor scenes in the following categories:

- Group the same locations together.
- Group scenes involving the same characters.
- Organise wide shots first, followed by mid shots, and then close-ups.

b.   Rearrange all indoor scenes in the following categories:

- Group the same locations together.
- Group scenes involving the same characters.
- Organise wide shots first, followed by mid shots, and then close-ups.

Now show the new version of the storyboard to one of your peers and ask them what the story is. The story will probably make very little sense in its present sequence. However, you will be left with a very useful tool for enabling you to shoot your video in the most efficient order. Bear in mind, however, that alterations to schedules can also occur on set, and therefore the continuity supervisor is still required to keep an eye on details such as costume, props, and character gestures and body movements.

Establishing the Production Team

So far, we have provided an overview of the production roles. There may be a certain amount of flexibility concerning team roles at different stages of your student project, with each individual's particular talent coming to the fore when needed. When it comes to an actual shooting day, however, it is always a good idea to have clearly defined roles.

If there is a team conference for each camera set-up, or if the sound recordist starts telling the camera operator how to frame the shots, the filming process will descend into chaos, and the team will become frustrated! Another good point to make here is that you should not try and do everything yourself. Make sure the team shares the weight of the project by allowing each member to contribute by following their assigned role.

The following exercise is an opportunity for you to practise on-the-job training in the roles that you are considering distributing in an actual production.

EXERCISE
The Record Routine

The record routine demonstrates the importance of allocating roles for a shoot, the formalities of the procedure, and highlights the benefits of logging shots, and observing continuity.

This exercise should be performed by the whole production team, and overseen by the appointed director. It entails recording a short interview between two people. You should keep it simple – for example, two questions answered in the duration of one to two minutes.

In order to carry out this exercise you will need the following equipment and materials:

- 1 camcorder and tripod;
- 1 external microphone with lead and boom pole;
- 2 lights and 1 reflector;
- 1 clapperboard with chalk and cloth;
- 1 clipboard with a shot log and pen for production assistant;
- 1 clipboard, pen and paper for the interviewer.

It may help to prepare a simple storyboard in advance of this exercise so that you can decide how many camera set-ups are needed. You could try a variety of camera angles as well as shot sizes. For example, you might want to include:

- long shot of the interviewer and interviewee – recorded for the duration of the whole interview;
- mid shot of the interviewer asking the questions;
- mid shot of the interviewee answering the questions;
- close-up of the interviewer asking the questions;
- close-up of the interviewee answering the questions;
- close-ups of 'noddy' shots – the interviewer and interviewee nodding as they listen to each other.

Discuss and assign the following roles:

- director;
- camera operator;
- clapperboard operator;
- sound recordist/boom operator;
- production assistant;
- continuity supervisor;
- lighting director;
- designer (sets, props, costume, make-up);
- interviewer;
- interviewee.

The director should organise crew members to take part in the record routine exercise. The production team should now work together to set up the shot. The design team should arrange the room so that unwanted furniture is put to one side. The director now decides how the scene is going to be filmed and will then instruct the crew. Each crew member should stick to their own task, determining what they need to do whilst the shot is set up. For example, the interviewer and interviewee will rehearse their questions and answers; the lighting director will set up the lights; the camera operator will set up the camera, and so on.

Once the director is satisfied that the team are ready, then it is time to go through the 'record routine':

- Director calls 'Silence on set!'
- Director asks 'Camera rolling?'
- Camera operator presses the record button and responds 'Camera rolling!'
- Clapperboard operator positions the clapperboard in front of the camera so that its contents can be recorded and calls out 'Scene 1, take 1!' then snaps the board shut: CLAP! They move out of shot.
- Director calls 'Action!'
- The shot is recorded.
- The director decides when the shot should end and calls 'Cut!'
- Camera operator presses the pause button.

The director and camera operator should review the shot and decide if another take needs to be recorded. If so, you should go through the record routine again, for example 'Scene 1, take 2'.

If another take is not needed, reposition the camera and continue by recording the following shot, 'Scene 2, take 1'. Once the director is satisfied with the recording of all the shots for the interview, the routine is over.

Once you have learned the 'record routine' you should aim to follow this every time you are on a shoot to maintain discipline and order.

Production Duties

So far we have looked at production team roles, and you have carried out a record routine exercise to help establish and define these roles. We will now look a little more closely at some production duties.

Location Scouting

Be practical and sensible about scouting for locations. If you have several locations planned for your production, keep them close together. Videos with a short running time usually do not need to have a multitude of locations – in fact, including too many may have a detrimental effect on the concise manner of your storytelling.

Your location scout needs to not only hunt for locations, but also consider the logistics for the crew, asking questions such as:

- Is the location convenient for reaching and completing the work in the scheduled time?
- Does the team have permission to film there?
- Is there a place to park vehicles nearby?
- Are there adequate refreshment and toilet facilities nearby?
- Is there a power supply?
- Will onlookers disrupt the production?

You should ask for permission to film in any location, explaining prior to the production who you are and why you will be recording there. Check for availability that cuts through red tape: If you plan to film in a shop, bar or other business premises, it might be a good idea to find out if one of your peers has a part-time job in such a place.

Planning to shoot scenes in a location that is situated 100 miles away from your place of study may not be very practical, especially when your cast and crew all have different timetables. Filming an interview by a fountain may provide a decorative backdrop, but it will be very difficult to record voices clearly next to the sound of running water. These are the considerations your location scout needs to make.

The location scout should conduct a 'recce' (reconnaissance) of any possible locations, and take photos to show to the producer. A typical location recce checklist will include details in a form like the one shown in Figure 8.1.

Location Recce Checklist				
Address and precise directions to the location of the shoot.				
Permissions to film required?	Yes	No	If yes, permission from whom?	
Times available and when not available.				
Electricity supply.				
Noise interference: air con, wind, etc.				
Obstructions: onlookers, traffic, limited space.				
Light: availability and need for extra.				
Other considerations.				

FIGURE 8.1
Location recce checklist form

Production Duties: Scheduling

Careful consideration needs be devoted to scheduling, so that your time is used effectively. Media-practice projects need to be scheduled alongside coursework and deadlines for other modules, and the timetables and availability of cast, crew, interviewees and other contributors all have to be factored in. If, for example, there is an occasion where the entire cast and crew need to be present for a particular scene, it is the producer's responsibility to gather all the many talents together and make sure that this process does not have to be repeated again. It is always a good idea to have a 'plan B' in case unsuitable weather disrupts the day's work, or if a member of the cast or crew cannot make it.

Because there are so many things to take into consideration from collecting equipment, journey times to and from locations, and times for refreshment breaks, it is a good idea to write all these down. The producer should create a production schedule, which is a calendar of the shooting dates and times. The production assistant follows this by distributing call sheets amongst the crew.

A call sheet will typically include the following information and you should adapt as appropriate to your own production:

Call Sheet				
Shooting day (number)	Call time	Day/date	Producer's name	Director's name

Scene number		Location		Cast

Cast member	Character or role	Make-up and costume	Setting

Special instructions and remarks

FIGURE 8.2
Call sheet

Production Paperwork: Health and Safety, and Risk Assessments

Health and safety legislation is a part of every workplace, and should not be overlooked during your production work. Acknowledging health and safety is part of your professional practice. In his book about health and safety in media production, Marco van Beek informs us that 'it is there for our benefit and protection, and has not been introduced as a personal vendetta by some dark overlord' (Beek, 2000: 13). He points out that we should 'never assume that we know more than someone else, but nor should we assume that they know more than us' (Beek, 2000: 13) and this is one of the reasons that health and safety should be observed in your productions – to identify any potential accidents before they happen.

Checking through health and safety forms is not only a matter of your own and your employer's/institution's legal protection, but is also good practice for the future, because any workplace that you enter after leaving your course will expect you to abide by health and safety rules. If you become self-employed, it will be up to you to put health and safety rules into place as part of your insurance.

Your place of study should have an approved risk assessment form that you can use. Alternatively, do some research into risk assessments and create your own form. A risk-assessment form should be completed for each different location you are working in. A typical form lists the potential hazards and might be set out as shown in Figure 8.3.

Risk Assessment Form					
Location		Date		Time/s	
Description of activity					
Names of production team members					
Names of additional persons					
Types of hazard (tick the hazards you are likely to encounter)					
Moving vehicles		Hot objects/ liquids		Working alone	
Moving machine parts		Noise		Geographical area	
Fall from height		Stairs		Weather	
Trips or falls		Chemicals		Heavy lifting	
Electrical		Dangerous animals		Shooting at night	
Risk evaluation (list the hazards ticked above and rate the level of risk below)					
Hazard		High	Medium		Low

(Continued)

111

State precautions to take having assessed the risks		
Hazard		**Precaution**
Name	**Signature**	**Date**

FIGURE 8.3
Risk assessment form

Once the potential risks have been identified on the form, your producer must assess the level of risk (usually in terms of high, medium and low), and then ensure that measures are made to avoid or control these risks. For example, if there is a danger of heavy lifting, make sure that your team shares the load, and uses a trolley to carry equipment. If there is a potential risk of trips or falls from electrical cables, make sure that they are firmly taped down to the floor.

The producer needs to ensure that every member of the production team has read through the risk-assessment forms, and signed and dated them to prove that they have assessed the risks.

Production Paperwork: Consent and Permissions

You should obtain consent from everyone that appears in one of your productions, including your friends and people from within the production team if they are doubling as actors or presenters. All professional productions require people to sign a 'release form' that proves that they have agreed to the recording or filming taking place, and that they do not object to it being used. Using release forms during your productions is a demonstration of your professional practice. It also enables your work to be shown publicly. Your place of study may be reluctant to upload any of your work to their website if there is no evidence that actors, presenters or interviewees have given written consent. Young people under the age of 16 and vulnerable adults will require a parent or guardian to sign a release form on their behalf.

Video shoots can be hectic and it is easy to overlook this important piece of administration in the heat of the moment. It is a good idea for the production assistant to ask the participants to sign forms before any shooting commences. If your team waits until after the shoot, it may be too late, especially if cast and crew have to dash off once the recording has finished. Make sure your participants sign a hard copy of the form. Do not copy and paste signatures onto an electronic document.

FAQs on Obtaining Consent

Q) If I am the producer and I am appearing in my own production, do I need to sign a consent form?

A) Yes – *you* know that you have agreed to appear in your own production, but the video may be shown publicly by someone who does not know that the actor and producer are the same person.

Q) I'm going to be filming in the middle of a crowded city. Do I need to ask every passer-by to sign a release form?

A) This is logistically impossible. In cases like this, use your common sense. If the scene includes one of your actors or presenters, make sure they are in the foreground, and that they are the focus of attention. If the shot is an establishing shot then there are no concerns as you will probably be filming a very wide shot in which people appear small and indistinct. If you are filming city scenes to use as cutaways in a non-fictional video then you could use a similar technique to some news reports that film crowd shots deliberately out of focus. The main point to be made here is not to deliberately single out members of the public by zooming in and filming them when they are unaware of it.

Q) I filmed a scene and forgot to get my actor/interviewee to sign a release form. What shall I do?

A) You could email an electronic version of the form and ask them to print, sign, scan it and email it back. Alternatively, as a last resort, ask them to send an email in which they agree to the footage being used. You can take a screen shot of this (or print it) and put it into your production log, classing it as written consent.

If your place of study does not already have a release form for you to use, then create your own and carry hard copies at all times during production. A typical consent form looks like the one shown in Figure 8.4.

Media Project Consent Form	
Name of production team	
Production team contact details (email address or main point of contact)	
Project brief/production title	
Date	

To be completed by the project participants: In signing below you are agreeing to your participation in the media project mentioned above and to it being edited and used in a variety of different contexts and to a number of different audiences.

Name	Signed by (must be signed by an adult on your behalf if you are under 16)	Contact (phone or email address)

FIGURE 8.4
Consent form

Production Paperwork: Copyright

Copyright laws can be a legal minefield, and can vary from country to country. The best way to prevent infringement of copyright is to avoid using any material that has not been created by you. An author is anyone who produces original work and this includes writers, composers, photographers, designers and musicians. *Re-recording a cover of a famous song does not avoid the issue of copyright!* It is the written composition of the tune that belongs to the writer, regardless of how it is subsequently performed. A recording of a written piece of work (for example, a recording of a written song) will also be subject to different copyright rules to that of the original work. *You can see how complicated this can get!*

If you need music for one of your projects, either find a friend or someone on your course who is a musician to record something for you, or use some simple music production software and compose your own. Alternatively, download some suitable music from a website that clearly provides copyright-free music.

Here is an important point to consider. Using an already-known tune as backing music for one of your videos can also be artistically detrimental to your production, and this is something that most students do not initially consider. If you use a well-known song or piece of music, the first-time viewer of your video will most likely identify with the tune, and in this case the music will take precedence, rather than the original parts of the production that you have created including the visuals.

If you want to enter your work into a festival or competition, a distributor or film programmer will want you to confirm that the music has been cleared. Using copyrighted music may prevent your work from being accepted. You should create a copyright log and keep a record of any images or sounds that you use in your productions and their copyright or non-copyright status.

Media Project Copyright Form				
Name of production team				
Production team contact details (email address or main point of contact)				
Project brief/production title				
Date				
Media form of material used (video, audio, image or other)	Description	Where obtained (web URL for example)	Copyright status	Details of permission to use

FIGURE 8.5
Copyright log

EXERCISE
Researching Rules of Copyright

To help you become more confident with this area of production, do some research into the rules of copyright, and answer the following questions. Keep a record of the answers for your future reference. You will probably need this information again after you graduate.

1. When does an 'authored' piece of work (a painting, song, book or film) become part of the 'public domain' and therefore free to copy?

2. Who out of the following holds the copyright to a film: the director, the screenwriter, the author of the dialogue or the composer of the specially created soundtrack score?

3. If I find images from online search engines, does this mean they are free to use in my productions?

4. If I want to produce a short film based on a Shakespeare play, will I be allowed to do this?

5. If I want to produce a video game based on *Peter Pan*, will I be allowed to do this?

6. If I find a piece of work that has no copyright information or © symbol attached to it, does this mean that I can use it in one of my projects?

7. Is remixing or editing someone else's work classed as 'derivative' and does this mean it is ok for me to use?

8. When I upload one of my own original videos to YouTube, who holds the copyright to that work?

9. What happens if I repeatedly infringe copyright (for example use someone else's music, or someone else's video clip) when uploading content to YouTube?

10. I intend to use someone else's work, but only for my personal use. Is this an infringement of copyright?

Summary

In this chapter you have learned some details about the different members of a production team and what their roles are. You have considered what duties need to be performed prior to and during production and the administration that this entails. Importantly, you have gained an insight into production ethics such as health and safety, gaining permission to film on location, and obtaining written permission from anyone who appears before the camera. These are all skills that can be considered as professional practice, improving your experience of organisation and planning. It is now time for you to produce!

Further Reading

For some practical guidance to support the organisation of your production, the following will be useful:

Beek, Marco van, 2000, *A Practical Guide to Health and Safety in the Entertainment Industry*, Cambridge: Entertainment Technology Press.

Fairweather, Rod, 1998, *Basic Studio Directing*, Oxford: Focal Press.

Gates, Richard, 2000, *Production Management for Film and Video*, Oxford: Focal Press.

Halligan, Fionnuala, 2012, *Production Design*, Lewes: Ilex.

Maier, Robert G., 1994, *Location Scouting and Management Handbook*, London: Focal Press.

Rabiger, Michael, 2003, *Directing: Film Techniques and Aesthetics*, Oxford: Focal Press.

Rowlands, Avril, 2000, *The Continuity Supervisor*, Oxford: Focal Press.

For more information on copyright rules, and to research the exercise above, visit the following websites:

copyrightuser.org

creativecommons.org

9

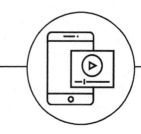

EDITING YOUR PROJECTS
Post-Production, Sound Design and Typography

After reading this chapter you will be able to:

- make connections between editing in theory and practice;
- consider how post-production editing constructs meaning in your media texts;
- design sound that creates a sense of three-dimensional space, and enhances your projects emotionally and culturally;
- consider the uses and effects of typography to augment your projects.

Introduction

In this chapter we discuss the post-production stage of your projects focusing primarily on video production. We take an analytical approach to editing and also look at the uses of sound and the uses of typography. We encourage you to analyse the editing of your own projects, just as you might if you were analysing an already existing text. In other words, we don't simply advise you *how* to edit a video, record sound or use typography. Instead, we ask you to think about *why* you might do this in a particular way, and what *effect* this may have on communicating an intended message for your audience. Ultimately, this will also enhance the quality of your media project work too.

As with the previous chapters, we also consider your work in the wider context of the media and creative industries. This will encourage you to think about your coursework in the context of professional practice.

First, however, let us examine some analytical approaches to editing that will inform your own practical work.

Post-production: Editing in Theory

Bordwell and Thompson argue that although 'everyone is somewhat aware of editing' it can still strongly 'shape the viewers' experience of [a] film', by 'manipulating time, space, and pictorial qualities' (Bordwell and Thompson, 2017: 217). Valerie Orpen considers editing to be 'an expressive strategy rather than a mere technique' (Orpen, 2009: rear book jacket). Editing can be considered as an *ideological* process that can persuade the audience to accept the preferred or intended reading of the text. As a media practitioner, it is useful to gain a theoretical understanding of how editing works to 'encode' meaning in a text, so that you can understand how best to communicate your intended message for the audience of your own projects.

The length that a shot is held in post-production can give priority to a particular character or viewpoint in a video. It can help to reveal, or conceal, certain pieces of information from the viewer. Editing can either appear conspicuous, or inconspicuous. For the former technique, the editing can be used to draw attention to other elements in the text – for example, in a music video, conspicuous editing can highlight the rhythm and pace of the music track.

The type of editing that appears inconspicuous or 'invisible' to the audience is, perhaps, the most common form of editing, but it is also the type that tends to take the most planning and skill to construct. Invisible editing or, rather, classical continuity editing is largely taken for granted, and this in itself demonstrates that it works ideologically, to 'disappear' from view. It is a formal language that viewers accept because it has become so familiar.

Classical Continuity Editing

Classical continuity editing is a form of editing that emerged in Hollywood in the 1920s and still exists today. It is a way of organising action across a sequence of shots that appears to be happening continuously within the same time and story space of the scene.

It may be the case that different shots in a scene were filmed hours apart, but continuity editing will construct the illusion that everything is happening in 'real time'.

Imagine a scene where a woman leaves her office at the end of a working day. A mid shot (MS) shows her rise from behind her desk as she looks into the near distance. A close-up (CU) of a clock is shown. We then see a long shot (LS) of the woman grabbing her coat and walking towards a door. The next shot is a long shot (LS) of her exiting the office block, walking onto the street, hailing a taxi. The audience has not seen the character's movements between the corridor and this scene, but they should be able to fill in the gaps.

The actions are continuous – from the woman rising out of her seat, to her entering the street – but the editing has cut out unnecessary 'dead time'. The final effect is to condense action and to give the viewer an idea about the spatial relations in the scene without it running in 'real' time. Constructing the sequence of her in the office to three separate shots including a cutaway of the clock also helps to condense the action and create interest.

Filming a scene, or sequence of actions in one wide or medium shot is one of the most common errors that often occurs in student productions, usually as a result of time constraints when filming. It may be quicker to film a continuous piece of action from one angle, but it is worth spending that extra bit of time to film a sequence several times from two or three different angles, and recording a sufficient number of cutaway shots. This will provide you with a better choice of shots when you are editing.

The use of a variety of different camera angles and shot sizes not only draws attention to the important parts of the 'story' within the text, and not only helps to construct the sensation of space and time, but it also maintains audience interest. A scene that is constructed from one wide shot lasting for a minute will not have the same dramatic impact as one constructed from a variety of shots and angles.

Film editor Walter Murch has defined a 'rule of six' which largely disregards the rules of classical continuity editing. His six criteria for editing are emotion, story, rhythm, eye-trace, the two-dimensional plane of the screen and the three-dimensional space of action (Murch, 2001: 18). For him, emotion comes first in priority, and three-dimensional space – constructed by continuity editing – comes last. Emotion and story and how the audience responds to these are paramount. Once you have learned how to use classical continuity editing, you can experiment with other forms of editing – such as the use of 'jump cuts' that we discuss later – but you should always try to ensure that the process of communication between story and audience is not disrupted.

EXERCISE
Filming the Same Sequence in One Shot, Then a Variety of Shots, and Piloting Different Test Edits

The simple fictional scenario outlined below might be the type of scene that establishes a new day before some important action takes place later in the story. Read the following scenario in preparation for filming it in the five different ways instructed below.

> A student enters a kitchen-dining space. He/she opens a cupboard, takes out a packet of cereal and places it on the kitchen counter. The person then walks to the sink and takes an empty bowl from the draining board. They walk to the fridge, take out a bottle of milk and go back to the cereal packet with their bowl and bottle of milk. They fill the bowl with cereal, pour milk onto it, and then walk to a sofa or kitchen chair and sit down to eat.

First version: film the whole sequence in one long take. If your room is big enough, try and frame the whole scene in LS (long shot) without moving the camera.

Second version: film the whole sequence in one long take, but allow yourself to move the camera. You could use a variety of pans, tilts, tracks and zooms to follow the action.

Third version: film the whole sequence in a variety of static shots on a tripod. Do not allow the camera to move. This might take a large number of camera set-ups. For example:

- Long shot (LS): Person enters a room.
- LS (different angle): Person opens cupboard and takes out cereal.
- LS (different angle): Person walks to kitchen counter.
- Mid shot (MS): Person places cereal packet on the kitchen counter then walks out of shot.
- LS: Sink area. The person then walks into shot and goes towards the sink, reaching for an empty bowl on the draining board.
- Close-up (CU): The bowl is seen being picked up.
- LS: The person walks to the fridge.
- MS: The fridge door is opened.
- CU: A bottle of milk is taken out of the fridge and the fridge door is closed.
- LS: The person walks back to the cereal packet with their bowl and bottle of milk.
- MS: They fill the bowl with cereal, then pick up the milk bottle.
- CU: Milk is poured onto the cereal.
- MS: The person puts down the milk bottle, picks up the bowl of food and turns to walk out of shot.
- LS: The person walks to a sofa or kitchen chair and sits down to eat.

Fourth version: try a combination of the second and third version. You can choose which parts of the action are most appropriate for short, static shots and other parts of the action where longer takes can be used, and where the camera might track or pan to follow the actor.

Fifth version: as a short sequence in a five- or ten-minute film, a relatively unimportant scene where someone is making breakfast like this can be condensed into a series of very familiar shots that serve to communicate this idea in a swift and economic way. With this in mind, you could condense the action as simply as follows:

- LS: Person enters room.
- MS: Person opens cupboard and takes out cereal.
- CU: Milk is poured onto bowl of cereal.
- MS: Shot of chair; person walks into shot, sits down and starts to eat.

Now edit the sequences together and play them back to your peers. Ask for some feedback on their preferred version of the scene. Make a note of the results and reflect on the following:

- How has time been condensed?
- How has the idea of three-dimensional space been constructed?
- How has dramatic impact been achieved?
- How could this be applied to non-fiction forms too?

Montage: The Kuleshov Effect

Another form of editing, which provides a contrast to continuity editing, is 'montage'. Bordwell and Thompson discuss the way that meaning can be constructed as a result of montage by the *Kuleshov effect* – sometimes referred to as the *third effect* – which was an experiment conducted by Lev Kuleshov who cut together 'neutral shots of an actor's face with other shots' such as shots of soup, nature scenes, a dead woman and a baby (Bordwell and Thompson, 2017: 226).

The result of the experiment was that audiences interpreted the neutral expression of the actor in different ways, depending on what the shot was juxtaposed with. For example, if the shot of his face was juxtaposed with food, then the sequence implied that he was expressing signs of hunger. Importantly, Kuleshov also demonstrated that it constructed the illusion that 'the man was reacting to nearby things that he could see' (Bordwell and Thompson, 2017: 226).

So, if you are worried about the acting abilities of a member of your cast, advise them that in screen-acting terms, 'less is more' – the audience's interpretation of the scene will largely be constructed by the juxtaposition of the shots in the final edit. If the actor looks at some tempting food, the audience will assume that the character is hungry.

FIGURE 9.1
This example of the Kuleshov effect demonstrates how two different meanings can be constructed by juxtaposing the same shot of the actor with two different images.

EXERCISE
Reconstruction of the Kuleshov Effect

Film a short sequence with one actor in one setting – such as a communal space (lounge/diner) in student accommodation. The sequence should consist of the following shots, and nothing else:

- Shot 1: Long shot (LS): person enters room, sits on sofa, and puts down bag.
- Shot 2: Mid shot (MS): person's body relaxes; they look across the room at something beyond the camera's view.
- Shot 3: Close-up (CU): of the person's face. It is quite expressionless and hard to 'read'.
- Shot 4: LS: person rises out of their seat and walks towards the space they were looking at, until they walk out of shot.
- Shot 5: CU: The person looks down at an object that is out of shot.
- Shot 6: (See below).
- Shot 7: CU: of face. The person looks at the object in their hands. Again their face is quite expressionless – as if they are deep in thought. Slowly their head rises and they look up into the middle distance/into thin air ...

For Shot 6: film several different cutaways. These should all be close-ups of an object that the person picks up off a table or kitchen work-surface that we see in their hands as a point of view (POV) shot; for example:

- someone else's personal diary;
- a utility bill for a vast amount of money;
- a mobile phone with an urgent message on it;
- a candid photograph of the main actor in an embarrassing situation;
- an expensive or luxurious gift.

Edit several versions of the sequence together, each with a different shot for Shot 6. Play one of each of the edited sequences back to your peers and ask them what they think the story is about and what the emotions of the main character are.

Think about ways that you might incorporate the techniques of continuity editing and 'the third effect', practised in the previous exercises in your own production work.

Editing in Practice

The previous exercises served to reveal how theoretical approaches to editing can be put into practice. The types of cutting we have looked at so far are classical continuity editing and montage. The following section will look at further types of cutting (including dissolves and fades) and how and when they are appropriate for use in your practical work.

Editing to Indicate Speed

It is possible that one of your video projects will include an action sequence such as a chase, or a sequence where a character is racing to get to a destination in a hurry. Rather than speeding up the action using the fast-forward in editing software, you can be much more sophisticated. For this type of sequence, it is a good idea to capture a series of many short shots of the character, or characters, at various stages of their journey. These shots can then be cut together to construct a technique that Monaco refers to as 'accelerated montage', whereby 'interest in a scene is heightened and brought to a climax through progressively shorter alternations of shots between two subjects' (Monaco, 2000: 218).

For example, in a series of alternate shots of two characters in a chase sequence, the first shots of each character might run for 2 seconds, with subsequent shots running for 1 second, and then 0.5 seconds. This type of 'accelerated montage' is not only an effective way of constructing excitement, but is also a good way of demonstrating your practical skills in editing. Rhythmic editing gives a much more convincing feeling of pace and movement than simply speeding up footage in post-production. With the latter technique the visual effect will draw attention to itself, whereas the skilled editing of 'accelerated montage' will work ideologically to involve the viewer in the action.

The Jump Cut

There are examples of editing in which the rules of classical continuity editing can be deliberately challenged. The jump cut is created when portions are removed from a long take without a change in camera angle. An example might be the editing of a shot of a glass of beer from full to empty – each successive jump cut shows the drink gradually going down in stages.

You can see how the use of a jump cut forgoes the rules of continuity editing. It is effective in certain types of texts such as music videos, because it draws attention to itself. It is a technique that you may wish to experiment with when you are producing texts that are less concerned with narrative, or in sequences where the form is given priority over the content.

The Dissolve

The dissolve is also often referred to as a 'cross-dissolve'. This is where two images overlap, rather than appear one after another, as they do in a straight cut. There are several reasons for using a cross-dissolve and these are motivated by the construction of meaning. This type of transition might indicate a change in time – for example, a scene that dissolves from day to night – or a change in location – for example, a scene that dissolves from indoors to outdoors.

Think carefully about the composition of the two shots that overlap. Try to avoid shots where two actors' faces overlap. Sound (which we discuss later in this chapter) should also mix between scenes during a cross-dissolve. This gives a better sense of continuity between the shots.

The Fade

The fade should be used for a specific purpose, which is usually to create a break between scenes or to indicate the start and end of a piece. For example, a fade-in from black usually indicates the beginning of the story, whereas a fade-out to black will confirm to the viewer that the story has come to an end. If a fade-out and fade-in occurs between scenes it is usually to indicate a change in time or a change in location. Always consider transitions such as fades and dissolves as a way of communicating a passage of time in the story or by providing a pause. Never use them gratuitously or without purpose.

Cutaways

Editing can be used to layer information rather than just to structure shots from end to end in a linear fashion. For example, in a fictional context, a cutaway can be used to insert extra detail in a scene, such as a shot of an object that a character is looking at. In a non-fiction piece, 'cutaways' or 'cover' shots can be used to mask a cut during an interview where you want to condense or abbreviate information. They can also be used to illustrate what an announcer, presenter or inter-viewee is talking about, or to gauge a reaction from someone listening on screen (in a 'noddy' shot), and therefore inform the viewer how to respond to the information.

With careful planning at the storyboard stage, or during filming, a series of shots can be gath-ered to use as cutaways. These can then be edited to illustrate what a presenter or interviewee is talking about, to give a sense of the environment in which the filming takes place, or simply to make for a more visually interesting scene.

Cutting to Sound

Sound can provide a valuable guide to how scenes should be edited. Cutting to sound (for exam-ple to music or voice-over) can be very effective. In editing to music you should first identify the beat, and use this as a guide. Cutting along to music can provide an alternative to 'invisible' con-tinuity editing because the editor may be able to use jump cuts, deliberately disrupted continuity and ambiguous imagery to create excitement, pace and variety in a sequence of images.

Introduction to Sound Editing

So far in this chapter, we have looked at the editing of images. We are now going to analyse the use of sound in audio-visual design. At first we might regard sound as secondary to the visual elements of film or video. We might assume that music is merely added afterwards for decoration or to emphasise mood. We might also take for granted that what we hear from the film or video is merely a recording that was made at the same time that the camera captured the visuals. This is often not the case. Sound is usually much more complex than we first assume it to be, and by understanding how sound works *ideologically* to construct ideas of space, continuity and culture, this will help to enhance the use of sound in your own media projects.

Sound and Ideology

Film scholars Bordwell and Thompson acknowledge that sound is perhaps the hardest technique to study and that it is 'often simply a background for our visual attention' (Bordwell and Thompson, 2017: 264). Similarly, Mary Anne Doane says that films are usually subject to the 'ideology of the visible' – that they rely on the audience to believe in what they see and accept it without question, and that this is due to the way that the standardised modes of film-making and presentation naturalises the finished product (Doane, 1985: 54). It is sound's 'invisibility' that contributes to the visual's power to work ideologically to make the audience believe in a film or video's construction of realism.

As a media practitioner, you can be just as selective about your use of sound, as you can select what shots to use in order to tell a story. Sound can be edited or added, which was not recorded at the same time as the filming.

The main function of sound, as with other film and video techniques (such as camera shots and editing), is to guide the viewer's attention to the important parts of information, or important parts of the story. You can use it ideologically to convince the audience that the sequence of shots they are witnessing are happening in 'real' time. Sound can flow across a series of edited images to mask abrupt cuts. The continuous sound across this series of cuts can include dialogue, the ambient or 'wild' sound of the room, and a music score.

You can design sound so that it constructs a sense of continuity across the shots, and helps to give a sense of realism: making it seem as though the shots all relate to each other and are taking place in the same space and moment in time. In reality, the shots may have been filmed hours or even days apart, and the dialogue might even have been dubbed on later during post-production. The sound never audibly stops and starts with each successive cut. If it did, it would sound jarring to the audience.

Volume Levels and Sound Perspective

Diegetic sound is sound that appears from within the 'story' space of an audio-visual text. Its opposite is non-diegetic sound; for example, a music soundtrack that is dubbed on to enhance mood, but that is not performed by musicians onscreen.

An important function that diegetic sound can suggest is a sense of spatial distance and aural perspective. The loudest sounds in the mix tend to suggest a sound source that is near, whereas soft sounds tend to suggest a sound source that is more distant. There are some exceptions to this rule, however, that are part of audio-visual technique.

For example, dialogue from the main characters in a fictional film tends to be at an even volume whether they are close to the camera (in a medium shot or close-up) or whether they are in a long shot. This is a characteristic of film and video production that audiences take for granted. It does not resemble real life, but is a convention of the storytelling. The main characters have to be heard clearly whether they are near or far from the camera. Imagine, for example, a scene that starts with two characters conversing in extreme long shot, walking along a hilltop, which then cuts to a medium shot of them carrying on with the conversation. The dialogue continues at the same volume between both shots, constructing audio-visual continuity.

Continuity of Sound

Petrie and Boggs highlight the usefulness of introducing diegetic sounds that emanate from sources in the story space of a film, but that are not seen on screen. This can be demonstrated, for example, with the sound of a closing door being used to indicate that 'someone has left the room even if we do not see an accompanying image' (Petrie and Boggs, 2012: 225). Extending the scope of the soundtrack in this way not only gives a sense of space beyond the frame, but also 'complements the image instead of merely duplicating its effects' (Petrie and Boggs, 2012: 225).

Using sound creatively in this way can liberate your camera operator and editor from having to visually represent every point of action. It is much safer to imply a vehicle crash by sound, for example, than it is to stage one using actual cars!

The use of sound can also provide a cue for something we are going to see in a forthcoming shot or scene. For example, we might hear the sound of a phone ringing off screen before we see it in the next shot. This is known as a 'sound bridge' and adds continuity between shots. Similarly, sound can smooth over transitions from one scene to the next. This is sometimes referred to as 'sound lapping' and is similar to the above function but helps us to anticipate the following scene rather than just the following shot. Think, for example, of an indoor scene coming to an end, but before the visuals finish the audience hears the sound of bird song or traffic, leading to the following outdoor scene. It is a very effective way of constructing audio-visual continuity from one spatial location to another.

Sound and Cultural Associations

It is also important to consider that sound has cultural associations. For example, sound can be considered in terms of gender. Think about a television news item where a woman who is speaking in her non-English speaking language has been overdubbed in English by a male translator or vice versa: the effect can appear rather strange, because the gender of the voice has been altered. In circumstances like this, the content of the information has taken priority over the gender of the two speakers, but it can disrupt the way that the viewer receives the information.

When recording a voice-over narration, you should think carefully about its cultural implications. If your media text is for a local audience, perhaps you should consider using someone who speaks with a local accent. Think about using someone who relates to the audience in terms of age, gender and racial identity. These aspects of constructing cultural identity with sound are an important aspect of character design.

Different genres of music (classical, hip-hop, doom metal) will appeal to different types of audiences. Music such as steel drums or a Hawaiian guitar can signify 'exotic' locations. Electronic music performed on a theremin or synthesiser has a similar function in science-fiction and horror texts. These 'other-worldly' sounds are used to represent outer space, or signify 'madness, fear and emotional distress' and help to rationalise or make sense of the unknown (Birtwhistle, 2010: 154–155).

Consider the use of music carefully in your own media texts, so that it creates mood and enhances the information, rather than detracts from it. If you are in doubt about where to use music, then relegate it to opening titles, end credits and montage sequences. During important pieces of dialogue or interviews it is best to avoid using music altogether, but if you do use it when someone is speaking, it should be very low in the mix. Considering which sounds predominate in the mix are part of what Doane refers to as the 'hierarchy of sound' (1985: 58).

Using Type and Typography in your Media-Practice Projects

Most audio-visual projects that you work on will include some form of typography or text. Online media relies heavily on communicating via a combination of written text and images, and the visual design and arrangement of the text is an important aesthetic element of any website. Film and video will also use some form of titles, and the design of these titles – particularly at the start of a video – is important in giving the audience clues about the genre, mood or atmosphere of the story that is to follow. White text on a black screen at the start of a video tells the audience nothing about the genre, mood or atmosphere of what is to follow.

Advertisements and poster designs will use typography to provide 'anchorage' for a photograph or illustration, or to further emphasise the message that is being communicated. Anchorage 'pins down' the meaning and helps the audience to understand the 'preferred reading'. You can use this technique in many audio visual forms.

FIGURE 9.2
Examples of anchorage using the same image but different straplines.

Consider the following regarding Figure 9.2:

- What makes the image speak for itself?
- How does anchorage enhance the meaning?
- How has anchorage been used to alter the way that the reader interprets the image?

Typography

It is important to consider the importance of anchorage in providing context to images, but the *style and arrangement* of the written text is also important in adding meaning, and this influences the way that audiences respond to type. For example, the typeface might help to denote 'authority', 'dignity' or a sense of 'casualness'. It may construct an air of approachability and informality, or it may be more formal. The size of the type can help to grab the audience's attention. It may appear to 'shout' from the page or screen, or its qualities might be subtler.

The choice of type (for example, the letters and font) and its arrangement (the typography) should both be considered carefully when constructing a preferred reading in your media-practice projects. The choice of typeface should be appropriate to the intended audience. These are the kind of questions you should be asking yourself as you explore the possibilities of typography:

- Is my media text aimed at fellow students or an external client?
- In what context will the media text be read?
- Is the media text informative or entertaining, professional or casual?

If you are creating 'transitional typography' – such as the animated 'idents' that are often used by television channels – you will need to determine how long your audience needs to read the text. Do you want the message to be decoded almost instantaneously, or do you want to challenge the reader and make them wait to decipher the message?

If you are using typography on a website, the audience will have more agency about how long they read a page for. If there is too much text, the reader may not be patient enough to scan all the information before navigating to another page. A similar thing may happen with your website if you use transitional typography that appears and evolves too slowly. The best way to test the timing of your typography – whether it is used on a website, presentation or video title sequence – is to read the words out loud and see if you can read it at a comfortable pace. Alternatively, get a friend to read it. Remember that your audience may be reading the text for the first time, so it should not be too fast, just as it should not be so slow that they lose patience and allow their attention to be diverted away from the screen.

In this chapter we have looked at the editing of images and sound, and the use of typography in audio-visual design. The following exercise is an ideal way of testing your skills in combining all of these elements.

EXERCISE
I Am a Camera Video

Use the following poem by Dziga Vertov as inspiration for a video, which you will film and edit. Your interpretation can be as literal or as avant-garde as you wish. Let your imagination run wild! Please note though – most successful videos should be trying to communicate an idea and not appear as a series of random images or 'visual wallpaper'.

I Am a Camera

I'm an eye. A mechanical eye. I, the machine, show you a world the way only I can see it. I free myself for today and forever from human immobility. I'm in constant movement. I approach and pull away from objects. I creep under them. I move alongside a running horse's mouth. I fall and rise with the falling and rising bodies. This is I, the machine, manoeuvring in the chaotic movements, recording one movement after another in the most complex combinations.

Freed from the boundaries of time and space, I co-ordinate any and all points of the universe, wherever I want them to be. My way leads towards the creation of a fresh perception of the world. Thus I explain in a new way the world unknown to you.

(Vertov, 1923, quoted in Berger, 1977: 17)

The following guidelines take into consideration much of what has been covered so far in the book, using camerawork and editing techniques to enhance meaning:

- The video should include a variety of shots including extreme long shots (ELS), long shots (LS), mid shots (MS), close-ups (CU) and extreme close-ups (ECU).
- It should include some camera movement including a tripod pan and tilt, and also some shots where the camera does not move, but the subject does.
- It should include diegetic and non-diegetic sound.
- It should include a deep soundtrack, for example layers of sound including wild sound, music, voice-over and sound effects.
- It should include some music, preferably copyright-free.
- You should think carefully about how you edit the images, following the soundtrack.
- The video should include some transitions such as jump cuts, dissolves, fades, or cutaways where appropriate.
- It should include titles, subtitles or other forms of onscreen text.

Once your edit is finished, analyse and reflect on the exercise.

List and explain the techniques that you used in order to construct your preferred reading.
Analyse how your use of these techniques was successful in creating your intended meanings.
What will you take from this exercise to inform your future media practice?

Summary

In this chapter we have looked in some detail at what happens to your media-practice projects in the post-production stages of your work, including editing, sound design and the use of typography. By discussing editing and montage in an analytical context, we have enabled you to think about the effects that this can have on a media text and audience, rather than simply thinking of post-production in terms of technical skills. You are now able to think about editing in terms of its construction of meaning, and how it works as a method of communication.

In the next chapter, we look at the distribution and exhibition of your work.

Further Reading

For a deeper appreciation about how theory can inform your post-production, you could read the following books:

Birtwhistle, Andy, 2010, *Cinesonica: Sounding Film and Audio*, Manchester: Manchester University Press.

Bordwell, David, and Thompson, Kristin, 2017, *Film Art*, New York: McGraw-Hill.

Doane, Mary Anne, 1985, 'Ideology and the Practice of Sound Mixing' in Weis, Elizabeth, and Belton, John, *Film Sound: Theory and Practice*, New York: Columbia University Press.

Orpen, Valerie, 2009, *Film Editing: The Art of the Expressive*, London: Wallflower.

Monaco, James, 2000, *How to Read a Film*, Oxford: Oxford University Press.

Murch, Walter, 2001, *In the Blink of an Eye: A Perspective on Film Editing*, Los Angeles, CA: Silman-James Press.

For more practical information on editing techniques try reading:

Bowen, Christopher J., and Thompson, Roy, 2013, *Grammar of the Edit*, Oxford: Focal Press.

For more detail on the uses and effects of typography you should look at the following:

Gonzales Crisp, Denise, 2012, *Typography*, London: Thames & Hudson.

Harkins, Michael, 2013, *Understanding Type*, London: AVA Publishing.

Hillner, Matthias, 2009, *Virtual Typography*, Lausanne: AVA Publishing.

Saltz, Ina, 2011, *Typography Essentials*, Gloucester, MA. Rockport

10

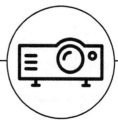

EXHIBITION AND DISTRIBUTION
Online Platforms, Festivals and Screenings

After reading this chapter you will be able to:

- promote and advertise your own work;
- exhibit and distribute your work through a variety of means;
- organise and manage events such as your own end-of-year showcase.

Introduction

At some point during your course, or, indeed, after your course, you may produce a piece of work that you wish to reach a wider audience, via a festival, exhibition or competition. Alternatively, you may wish to disseminate your work online to advertise your skills and services for potential employment. This chapter will give you an insight into some possible ways to get your work out there. It will also provide you with information about organising your own showcase. Let's start by considering how to promote your work online.

Sharing Media Online

One of the best ways to practise reaching an audience is by sharing your video online using various social media platforms. Chapter 12 contains useful information on constructing a portfolio of your work and for performing a 'social media makeover'. This will enhance your employability and enable you to be ready for the world of work. In this chapter, however, we will introduce you to thinking about how you might disseminate specific projects online.

Depending on your particular focus you should start by choosing the most appropriate platform with which to store and share your work; for example, video-sharing sites, audio-sharing sites, image-sharing sites or blogs. Linking these to social-media platforms to build up interest is the best starting point in getting your work out there for potential viewers, listeners and readers, and it's free!

Media on video-sharing sites can either be set to be viewed by anyone, or to be viewed by people with a direct online link to the video, or to people with a password. It depends on your aims. Do you want the video to be seen by as wide an audience as possible? Or do you only want to share it with potential employers or festival programmers? Is it a single production, or part of an online series?

It is important to highlight here that sharing work online in this way is not necessarily just a way of impressing potential employers – it can also become a full-time paid job if you make a success of it.

The phenomenon of vlogging has taken off considerably in recent years. Successful vloggers have built careers on advertising revenue from 'pop-up' ads at the beginning of their videos, or have worked with famous brands in order to build an audience of multiple thousands of viewers.

Vlogging is potentially simple and inexpensive because you can start off by filming your vlogs in a domestic space with basic equipment. It is also a way of developing presenting skills and networking with fellow vloggers. However, in order to be a successful vlogger you must have the right sort of on-screen personality and niche selling point in order to attract viewers. For every successful vlogger, there are countless people who have started and then fallen by the wayside. Ideally, once viewers find your vlog your work has to convince them to subscribe to your channel for frequent visits.

Vlogging is something you could explore while you are still a student. Even if you do not transform this into a full-time career, you will have built up your confidence and learned valuable skills in communicating with an audience. These are the types of skills that will make you appeal to future employers.

Using Social Media to Advertise Your Work

Using social media is an excellent way to advertise your work. If you already use social media as a way of interacting with friends, then it is worth creating a separate account *specifically* for your work, and keeping the content professional. Whether you are producing a regular vlog or a single video, then you could create an account solely for the vlog or video itself during the early stages of the project, and post updates on social media about your progress.

Using Twitter provides you with a test for writing succinct pieces of prose. (This will be useful later in the chapter when we look at writing a synopsis for a press release.) Because each tweet is allowed a limited number of characters you are required to write as economically as possible. However, Twitter also enables you to share images and short video clips too. For example, you can tweet stills from a video, or shots of work taking place behind-the-scenes and in post-production. You could post updates about any screenings that are going to take place, or post links to the video or a trailer on your video-sharing account.

Use hashtags '#' in tweets about your work to help advertise it (for example, #Introducing MediaPractice). If someone comes across one of your tweets, they can follow the hashtags to find a thread of previous tweets about your work.

Step-by-step Guide to Tweeting your Projects

The following scenario gives advice on how you could promote a video production with a view to it ultimately being shared online or screened publicly at a festival or competition. If you are working as part of a bigger team you could assign these duties to a production assistant or someone particularly interested in developing skills in PR. Adapt the guide as you see fit.

Once your idea for a production is established, set up a Twitter account to advertise your work. Now compose some tweets on the following topics:

- Pre-production:
  - Announce that you are working on a forthcoming project. Name the production (even if it is a working title) and create a hashtag for it.
  - Tweet that you are on the look-out for cast and crew members. Early tweets such as these will create interest and attract like-minded 'followers'. Include hashtags such as #castingcall #crewing #filmcrew.
  - When you acquire any cast or crew members, announce this in a tweet and '@' them. Include photographs of them, with their permission.
- Production:
  - Tweet a series of 'behind-the-scenes' shots of your production in progress. These could include shots of the actors on location. The same publicity stills could be used in a press pack if you intend to enter the production into a festival or competition. Continue to use hashtags for your production.
- Post-production:
  - Tweet about the editing stages of the production and an estimated or definite date for its completion.

When the production is finished, Tweet about the online premiere, or any of the production's screenings. Use Twitter to invite people by '@' them or sending them direct messages. However, do not create 'spam' by posting numerous messages and targeting strangers – this may be a breach of Twitter's regulations. Tweet links to your online trailer, and keep up to date with news on further screenings, or on your following productions.

Your Twitter feed will provide an insight into your work ethic for future employers. However, it is worth noting the following tips:

- Don't tweet too often. First, you do not want to annoy people with too many narcissistic updates. Besides, if you have many thousands of tweets on your timeline, future employers will think that you never have time to do any work!

- Do not mix your social life and professional life on your social-media feeds. Keep a separate account for sharing with your friends.

Festivals

It is worth doing a bit of research during your course to find out about any exhibitions or festivals that take place annually and when the deadline dates are for entering any work. This will enable you to consider entering a piece of your coursework if it fulfils the festival's submission criteria.

Elliot Grove provides a useful insight into how some of the major and mini-major film festivals are organised, but tends to play down the value that smaller film festivals have. He says that local festivals run by 'one or two people … attract local press, but very few industry people' (Grove, 2006: 283). Do not let this somewhat defeatist attitude put you off. Many small film festivals welcome newcomers, or films by young people, and have award categories aimed specifically at identifying new talent. Small, local events and screenings are a way of gaining exposure and receiving valuable feedback about your work. Even if you do not win an award, having one of your productions screened at a film show or festival is a huge achievement that you can add to your CV.

There are festivals with themes, festivals that challenge you to produce a short film in 24 hours, and festivals that stipulate that the films should be no longer than one minute. Remember, the shorter your film or video is, the better chance it usually has of being screened during a festival programme, especially if the festival's running time is only for a couple of hours.

If your video runs for several minutes, you may want to think about creating a trailer for it. Select some of the highlights from your video – particularly dynamic shots with plenty of action – and use this as a way of generating further interest.

The entry requirements for festivals differ. Some charge an entrance fee, whereas others are free. Many festivals prefer you to send a link to a video online so that they can preview it, and then download the file if they choose to screen it.

Publicity stills from productions are a useful way of promoting your work. It is always recommended that you make a record of your own work in progress throughout a media project. These provide a record of yourself in practice. If you plan to disseminate your work, either online, or to enter into a film festival, it is a good idea to capture a selection of publicity stills and 'behind-the-scenes' images during production.

Festivals are not just for film-makers. There are also competitions for new screenwriters, and festivals that give screenwriters the opportunity to 'speed-pitch' their ideas. Radio is also a particularly good market for new pieces of drama. It is worth spending some time doing some research in order to find a festival that is right for you.

The following exercise will enable you to research festivals and competitions, and find out more about the festival circuit.

EXERCISE
Researching Festivals and Competitions

Search online using keywords such as 'short film festival', 'young people's film competition', 'scriptwriters' competition'. Use other search criteria such as genre and subject matter. Identify and choose one example that is of interest to you.

Ask yourself:

- Is there a programme or running order from the previous year's festival?
- How often does the event run? Is it annual, biannual, or is it the first time it has run?
- How long is the duration of the whole programme? Does it only run for a couple of hours, or a few days?

Make a note of any categories that each festival/competition may have; for example:

- best newcomer;
- best non-fiction;
- best fiction;
- best animation.

What category is your work most suited to?

Make a note of entry requirements such as:

- age restrictions;
- duration or running time;
- entry fees;
- copyright status;
- provision of synopsis, cast and crew list;
- provision of publicity stills;
- technical specifications.

Look out for previous entrants' work online. What further insight into the festival does this give you? Keep a list of these facts and entry requirements for future reference.

Writing a Synopsis

Festival requirements often ask you to summarise your film entries with synopses of differing lengths; for example, a longer one – of approximately 150 words – for the actual entry form, and a shorter one – of 50 words – for the film programme. Very brief 'loglines', as we explain later, are also useful for advertising your projects.

You should practise writing short summaries of your work in preparation for entering into competitions and festivals. The following exercise gives you an idea of how challenging this can sometimes be. It also helps you to develop a knack for being succinct and precise when describing your work. Therefore, it is a writing skill that can be applied to other uses, such as CV writing and job applications where you need to say as much as you can, in as few words as possible.

EXERCISE
Writing a Short Synopsis for a Film Festival

Free writing: write a summary of your video (fiction or non-fiction) as swiftly as possible. Don't be precious at this stage. Write whatever comes into your head, and do not worry about the word count. You can probably fill one side of A4 with this description.

You can include information such as:

- who the main characters or participants are;
- where and when the video is set;
- for fiction projects: a plot summary with a beginning, middle and end;
- for non-fiction projects: an outline of content from beginning to end.

150-word synopsis: count the words of your summary above and read through it. How succinct is it? What superfluous elements can be edited out? Pick out the most important elements and use them in a summary of no more than 150 words. Try and use as near to 150 words as possible. You will find that it is quite a test.

50-word synopsis: now, try and edit out another 100 words so that you are left with no more than 50 to summarise your video.

The logline: write a logline of between 10 and 20 words that summarises your video. For this you will want to choose a phrase with maximum impact and as few words as possible that entices the casual reader and makes them want to find out more about your work.

Writing a Press Release

The previous exercise will provide you with some valuable experience and material for writing a press release for your work. A press release should ideally be kept to one side of A4, and definitely no more than two sides. It should include some brief information on the people involved in the project as well as details about the content of the production (for example a synopsis). It should also state where and when your production will be seen and your contact details for further press information.

Remember that a journalist may receive a pile of press releases every day, and although they may be on the look-out for stories, they will often be working to tight deadlines, so if the purpose of your message is not clearly communicated, the reader is likely to bin it and move onto the next potential story. Therefore, your press release needs a clear heading that grabs the reader's attention, and should be written in no more than five short, snappy paragraphs that use keywords – do not waffle!

It may be a good idea to include an image somewhere near the top of the page. The press release should be delivered as a Word document or PDF. You should also include a release date or what is often referred to as an 'embargoed' date, so that the journalist does not publish the information until the most appropriate time.

You should consider who the potential audience of your project is, and whether this can be matched to the audience of a magazine, newspaper, website or festival. Think about whether the audience is local, national or international when distributing your press release. The template in Figure 10.1 should help you.

Events Management: Organising Your Own Screening

One alternative to entering your work into festivals and competitions is to organise *your own* screening. If you are thinking about going into events management for a possible career, then organising your own screening is a great opportunity for you to add the experience to your CV. It is also a good way of inviting potential employers to see your work.

Managing an event can take months to prepare, so it is a good idea to look ahead and consider all the requirements and logistics that need arranging long before the date of the event approaches.

In the early stages of events management there may only be a handful of organisers involved – yourself and your peers. You are best advised to gather a committee of peers to organise the event. Set objectives such as the scale of the event (how many people will be invited), and when and where it will take place.

When it comes to planning, decide how many volunteers will be needed to help out on the actual day. Duties may include a receptionist to welcome the guests and ask them to sign a visitors' register; ushers to guide people to their seats or show them to toilets and exits; and hospitality staff to supply refreshments. You may also want someone to control the lighting, someone to be in charge of AV duties, and also two people to act as the 'masters of ceremony' (MCs). These could be local dignitaries, alumnae, students on your course or members of staff.

Organising a screening takes a lot of time and effort, but it is an excellent way of demonstrating your skills in teamwork, team leadership, communication and organisation – all of which you should have developed during your time as a media-practice student.

You will find that managing an event is a great networking opportunity, as well as a good way to celebrate all your efforts at the end of your production. To organise the event, you should create a plan in both electronic and hard copies that everyone involved has access to. The outline in Figure 10.2 will work as your guide:

Press Release

(You need to make it clear that this is a press release, so it is worth writing these words at the top of the page!)

Embargoed until: Date/Month/Year

HEADING

Subheading

image

Paragraph 1: Introduction: Overview of production – who is involved, what it is about, where it will be seen, and when.

Paragraph 2: More detailed information on the content of paragraph 1

Paragraph 3: A quote that endorses your production/event

Paragraph 4: Extra information that either elaborates on the quote or includes further details on the production/event

Paragraph 5: Conclusion: Summary of all of the above

Note to Editors:

- This section should include any extra information such as biographical details of the people involved, or information about the organisation/s involved. You can also include links to a relevant website here.

Contact details:

Your name

Preferred contact address (email/social media)

Phone number *(This is in case the journalist wants to contact you for further information.)*

FIGURE 10.1
Press release template

Events Management: How to Organise a Screening

The templates in Figure 10.2 cover all duties and tasks before, during and after an event. Depending on the size and type of event, you might not perform all these duties and tasks, but this list will give you an idea of the organisation that event planning involves.

Pre-event Planning					
Name of event					
Names and contact details of people in event management committee					
Names and contact details of other contributors					
Duties/tasks	Person responsible	Who else to contact (e.g. brief provider, actors, participants, room, catering)	Contact details (email/ phone no.)	Deadline for performing task	Tick when task is completed
Find a date/dates for the event					
Determine the running time of the event					
Determine the running order (if it is an event such as a showcase of multiple projects)					
Design the floor plan/ layout					

(Continued)

Decide how many people should be invited to attend					
Find a suitable location for the event					
Do a risk assessment of event space, check safety exits and toilet facilities					
Check disabled access of event space					
Check AV facilities of event space					
Book the room/s					
Determine the budget for the event					
Order any special furnishings, lighting or decorating materials for the event					
Order refreshments/ catering and book delivery time and venue for these					
Design and print posters to advertise event					
If event is to be photographed, book and brief photographer					
Compose electronic invitations including event poster					
Invite guest speakers/ MCs					

Write script for event/ introductory speeches					
Write a press release for the event. Send to local press/student magazine/student radio/student TV					
Create a social media account/page for the event and a hashtag to advertise it. Post updates in the build-up to the event					
Send out invitations (including RSVP for car parking/dietary requirements/special needs and access). Book parking spaces					
Create register of attendees					
Arrange furniture/ decorate space/hang signs					

During the Event		
Tasks	**Person responsible**	**Contact details**
Open the event space		
Make final arrangements of furniture/lighting		

(Continued)

Hang signs/A-boards/banners		
Brief stills photographer		
Car-park attendant to direct guests to parking space and event space		
Receptionist to receive guests and take register		
Ushers/caterers to pour refreshments during event		
Ushers to guide guests to seats		
Guest speaker to make opening speech		
MCs to introduce event, go through housekeeping announcements, and other speeches		
Person to perform AV duties during event		
Guest speaker to make closing speech		
Ushers/caterers to serve buffet/ refreshments at end of event		
Post updates on social media accounts during event using your hashtag		

After Event			
Tasks	Person responsible	Deadline for performing task	Tick when task is completed
Tidy up buffet/refreshments			
Take down signs, A-boards and banners			
Post updates about the event on social media accounts using your hashtag			
Upload event photos to social media accounts			
Write a follow-up press release for the event. Send to local press/student magazine with any photographs taken of the event			
Send out thanks to the guests and speakers, and inform them of any follow-up publicity in the press and social media pages			

FIGURE 10.2
Events management planning template

As you can see from the templates, organising an event can be a major feat of patience, planning and endurance. But the rewards will be plentiful when it all runs to plan. You can add the experience of event planning to your CV. What better way could there be of proving your organisational skills to potential employers?

Summary

In this chapter we have considered different ways to publicise, distribute and exhibit your work. This chapter has also helped to boost your level of employability. The writing exercises included here will assist you in honing written communication skills. These are not only useful for writing press releases and online profiles of your work, but will also be useful for writing your CV and personal statement when applying for jobs in whatever field of work you pursue after leaving your course.

In the following chapter we explore ways of critically reflecting and analysing your work.

Further Reading

We recommend these books for further information on some of the topics covered in this chapter:

Bowdin, Glenn, Allen, Johnny, O'Toole, William, Harris, Robert, and McDonnell, Ian, 2006, *Events Management*, London: Elsevier.

Parks, Stacey, 2007, *The Insider's Guide to Independent Film Distribution*, Oxford: Focal Press.

11

EVALUATING YOUR MEDIA PROJECTS
Critical Analysis and Reflection on Media Project Work

After reading this chapter you will be able to:

- assess and evaluate your completed media text;
- make links between media and cultural theory and your own practice;
- assess and evaluate the teamwork that took place during the project;
- critically reflect on and analyse your own work and your working practices;
- make links between your media project work and your future employability.

Introduction

We have seen in previous chapters that many of the skills developed through media-practice project work will be beneficial for careers in the media and creative industries. We will see in this chapter that critical reflection and analysis skills are a useful part of any educational media project, but also essential for enhancing your employability.

We will begin with a critical analysis of the media text you have created, where media theory can be used to analyse your product. We then move on to look at the process of your project, highlighting the importance of analysing teamwork and team dynamics. Finally, you are encouraged to reflect on your individual contribution to the project.

We will look at the different ways in which you can present such reflective work, in the form of essays and reports. Some suggested essay titles and questions are also provided here as a springboard for your written work.

Critical Analysis of a Media Text

We will start, then, with considering how to analyse and evaluate the quality of your completed media text. We focus on a video in this case but this could be transferred to other media forms if necessary. The aim is to attempt a deep critical analysis of the video you have produced within your team. These exercises will help you to uncover some of the techniques you have used to communicate meaning and to assess the success of this.

EXERCISE
Critical Analysis of the Mise en Scène of a Completed Video

Start by creating a screenshot/still from your completed video. It should be a wide shot, set in a specific setting and it should contain at least one person. Analyse the following elements of audio-visual communication that have been covered in the previous chapters of this book. You could refer back to refresh your memory for some of the elements and there is some suggested wider reading at the end of this chapter:

- The design of the setting.
- The design of the props.
- The design of the people – through character type and costume, and the directing of gesture, posture and proxemics.
- The design of the lighting.
- The use of colour.
- The use of visual effects.
- The design of the typography.

For each of the elements above:

1. Describe each of the elements in your screenshot/still.

2. Analyse how each element communicates meaning, and why.

3. Make suggestions for improvement to each if you had the opportunity to work on the project again.

In the example in Figure 11.1 we focus on the analysis of the design of people. The screenshot/still is from a documentary about student poverty and their use of food banks.

FIGURE 11.1
Example of a screenshot for a critical analysis of the design of people

Example:

1. Describe the element in your screenshot/still.

    the design of the people (through character type and the use of costume, gesture, posture and proxemics)

Two young women in their early twenties. They are wearing casual clothes and appear neat and tidy. One is wearing ripped jeans and the other a puffer jacket. The character who is approaching the bench has a bag slung over her shoulder. The woman sitting on the bench has closed body language. She is looking directly at the person approaching her and frowning. They are about to have an encounter.

2. Analyse how each element communicates meaning, and why.

We chose young women in their early twenties to represent the student population that the video is about. The clothes make them come across as typical students. The ripped jeans could denote poverty, but could also be read as a fashion statement. The personal prop (the leather shoulder bag) denotes wealth and style. The body language and proxemics communicate a tension between the two people which is what the video goes on to show. The fact that the woman with the bag is standing over the other implies dominance and superiority. She is the interviewer for the video.

3.   Make suggestions for improvement to each if you had the opportunity to work on the project again.

We cast members of our project group in the roles of students who are experiencing hardship because we couldn't find anyone else willing to be on camera about this. If we had the opportunity to make this video again we would cast a male and female to make it more representative of the student population. We would have cast people who are really experiencing poverty as students rather than actors. This would give the video more credibility, make the message more convincing and gain the sympathy of the viewer. We inadvertently created a tension between the two characters due to their body language and would alter this to make them appear more equal.

The above exercise encourages a close analysis of the mise en scène of a still from your project. The following exercise is similar, but it requires an analysis of the audio-visual elements of your project.

EXERCISE
Critical Analysis of the 'Grammar of the Shot and Edit'

Refer to a final copy of your completed video for this exercise. You could use screenshots or a storyboard with notations, or short video extracts to illustrate your analysis. Refer back to Chapters 7 and 9 to refresh your memory for some of the techniques listed. There is also some wider reading given at the end of this chapter. Some of the points below are elaborated in Bowen and Thompson's *Grammar of the Shot* (2009) and *Grammar of the Edit* (2013). Analyse your video in relation to the following audio-visual elements:

- **Motivation** – the part of the shot that gives the editor a reason to cut to another shot. For example, who the text is about, where they are and what they are doing.
- **Information** – each new shot should have new information for the audience, so analyse the new information contained within the shot you are analysing.
- **Composition** – analyse the use of framing and perspective in the shot and specifically how this is used to communicate meaning.
- **Sound** – analyse how you have used voice-over, dialogue, music, sound effects, ambient or wild sound to enhance the message.

- **Camera angle** – describe and analyse how you have used different camera angles.
- **Shot size** – describe and analyse your use of different shot sizes.
- **Composition** – describe and analyse how you have used techniques of 'looking' or 'nose room' and 'walking room' to enhance communication.
- **Camera movement** – describe and analyse your use of motivated camera movement such as pan, tilt, cant, track and zoom to enhance communication.
- **The cut** – describe and analyse how you have cut from one shot to the next using continuity editing to help communicate meaning.
- **Jump cuts** – describe and analyse how removing a portion of footage from a long take without a change in camera angle has been used.
- **The dissolve** – describe and analyse your use of a dissolve where two shots overlap in a cross-dissolve/gradual transition.
- **The fade** – analyse your use of a fade in from black or out to black.
- **Cutaways** – describe how you have used layering information to illustrate action or a point in more detail through the use of cutaways.

For each of the criteria for analysis above, think about the following:

1. Describe how the audio-visual element is used by picking out an extract from your completed video.
2. Analyse how the element communicates meaning, and why.
3. Make some suggestions for improvement if you had the opportunity to work on the project again.

Assessment and Evaluation of a Completed Video

You can use this critical analysis of the text in the exercises above to move on to assess and evaluate your completed media text. This exercise focuses on a video project but could be adapted for other media forms. Involvement in assessment and evaluation, including peer evaluation, is a feature of media practice and it is a useful skill to develop for your employability.

EXERCISE
Assessment and Evaluation of a Completed Video

This exercise will give you some suggested criteria for assessment and how these might be used for a deep evaluation of a video you have produced. Focus on your completed video (or one made by a peer group) as a basis for evaluation and assessment. Complete the form in Figure 11.2.

Assessment and Evaluation Form							
Assessment Criteria	Comments	Assessment					
		Poor	Fair	Good	Very good	Excellent	Out-standing
The original idea – its appropriateness to the brief given, its originality and quality, how much the idea shines through in the completed video.							
The content of the video – the depth of treatment, the level of research and understanding, its suitability to the media form used, its level of detail, its balance of form (style) and content.							
The form of the video – the pace and rhythm, its timing and impact, its sequencing of shots, its use of the techniques and conventions of audio visual communication.							
The technical accomplishment – demonstration of camera, sound recording and editing skills through the completed video.							
The audience and market for the video – the appropriateness of the text to who will watch it and where and how it will be viewed.							

FIGURE 11.2
Assessment and evaluation form for a video

In the second column, for each of the criteria, offer an example or evidence in the comments section. For each of the assessment criteria listed in the first column, think about what level each should be awarded for the video you are assessing using the assessments below:

- Outstanding – 80 per cent and above.
- Excellent – 70–79 per cent.
- Very good – 60–69 per cent.
- Good – 50–59 per cent.
- Quite good – 40–49 per cent.
- Poor – 40 per cent and below.

Critical Analysis and Reflection

Having assessed and evaluated your completed media text in the exercises above, you should have started to create a distance between you and the text. It is this distance that we will move on to examine when thinking about critical reflection. Opportunities for critical reflection are an essential aspect of learning from media practice. We will begin by looking at ways of reflecting on the completed media text (or *product*) and we then move on to reflecting on the team and project work (or *process*) and the part you played in it.

Reflective Essays and Analysis

A reflective essay can help you contextualise your media project work with the whole of your degree course. Such an essay will be less concerned about *what you did*; instead it will be more about your project in the context of media theory, cultural studies theory or film studies. You might approach the analysis of your own work by using cultural studies *methodology*. Do not be intimidated by this term. Methodology merely refers to the research methods you will use to analyse your work.

For example, you might analyse your practical work in the context of debates around representation, identity, gender, and so on. Or you might write an essay that is linked more to media forms; for example analysing your work in the context of a particular genre, or analysing your use of narrative structure, or cinematography. The important thing to stress here is that using methodology like this helps you to be more analytical about your work and less descriptive. It creates some sense of distance. We will offer some suggested areas of focus and essay questions below, followed by some guidelines for writing such a critically reflective essay.

Essay Questions for Critical Analysis of the Product

Some of the following essay questions suggest ways that you can use film and media theory as a framework for analysing your own work. They refer to topics that have been introduced to you previously in this book. In order to satisfactorily answer the questions, you should first demonstrate your understanding of the relevant theoretical arguments before applying them to your own product.

Some of the questions include references to guide you to relevant reading, but we recommend that you also do some wider reading in preparation for these essays. A close textual analysis of your own product as you have done in the exercises above will also help to illustrate what you say.

The questions below are listed in sections around themes and aim to enable you to focus on specific areas of theory rather than being too broad in your approach. You might want to refer to the chapter each question relates to for wider reading and a starting point.

Questions on audiences: the following essay questions relate to Chapter 4 of this book where you can also find some suggested wider reading to help add depth to your work.

- Explain how you aimed to encode a 'preferred reading' in your media text, but how there may be the possibility of alternative readings by audiences that the text is not directed at.

- Referring to the uses and gratifications model, analyse how your audience will use your text in any of the following ways: for information, to construct personal identity, for integration and social interaction, or for entertainment.

Questions on writing: the following essay questions relate to Chapter 5 of this book where you can also find some suggested wider reading.

- Bordwell and Thompson say that 'Most scholars agree that no genre can be defined in a single hard-and-fast way' (Bordwell and Thompson, 2017: 328). Examine how your own work might be defined by genre.

- Write a critical analysis of the narrative structure of your video referring to Todorov's theory of narrative structure. Does it follow Todorov's five stages, or is his theory challenged by your work?

- Analyse your video using Raskin's seven parameters for short film (Raskin, 2002).

- Sheila Curran Bernard argues that 'creative nonfiction is narrative, it always tells a good story' (Curran Bernard, 2016: 4). How can your documentary (or other non-fictional form) be considered as a form of 'storytelling'?

Questions on the mise en scène: the following essay questions relate to Chapter 6 of this book where you can also find some suggested wider reading.

- Examine the issue of representation in your media project focusing on one of the following topics: gender, ethnicity, sexuality or age.

- Explain whether you deliberately challenged stereotypes in your media text, and how you achieved this.

- Affron and Affron (1995) identify five levels of design intensity for film settings. Discuss the way that you approached the design of the settings in your media production, and analyse their meanings

- Sarah Street asserts that 'film costumes not only relate to the characters who wear them but also to the audiences who watch them' (Street, 2001: 7). How did you consider the significance of costume design in your own media project?

Questions on the technical and formal elements: the following essay questions relate to Chapter 7 of this book where you can also find some suggested wider reading.

- Explore the way that light and shade helps to enhance communication in your project. Analyse the way that you manipulated light through its intensity, its direction, and through the use of filters.

- Patti Bellantoni (2012) highlights the storytelling functions of colour. How did you design the use of colour in your video, and what was its effect?

- Analyse the way that composition and framing has been used in your work to draw the audience's eye to the important parts of the image; how it evokes intimacy or distance; and how you have deliberately included and excluded certain elements.

- Explain the significance of camera movement in your video production. Analyse the way that you encouraged viewers to 'become involved in a character's physical or psychological sensations' with the use of pans, tilts, cants and tracking shots (Pramaggiore and Wallis, 2011: 144).

Questions on post-production: the following essay questions relate to Chapter 9 of this book where you can also find some suggested wider reading.

- Valerie Orpen considers editing to be 'an expressive strategy rather than a mere technique' (Orpen, 2009). Analyse the construction and organisation of meaning in your own production.

- Classical continuity editing is largely taken for granted, and works ideologically, to 'disappear' from view. How does the editing of your own text (a) appear invisible, and (b) are there any instances where you had difficulties in constructing continuity with your editing?

- Doane says that films have a 'hierarchy of sounds' which gives dialogue primary consideration, with sound effects and music as secondary (1985: 58). Scrutinise the soundtrack of your own media text.

- Consider the cultural significance of sound in your media text. Analyse its construction of authority, authenticity and other factors such as the significance of age, gender and ethnicity.

- Gonzales Crisp asserts that 'Text elements always denote something – that is, have a literal meaning – and also always connote additional meanings by evoking associations' (Gonzales Crisp, 2012: 33). In reference to your own work, how does the use of typography both denote and connote meaning?

Writing Your Own Essay Title

Essay questions will usually be set by your tutor. However, in some instances – such as a research project or dissertation – it may be the case that you are required to write your own essay question that focuses on a critical analysis of the media product you have created. Once you have decided on the focus of the essay you need to define the research question/s and therefore the essay question itself. Here are two examples of essay titles, which students wrote when critically analysing their video projects:

- 'The Representation and Role of Women Within the Horror Film I Produced and the Concept of the Monstrous Female'
- 'To What Extent Does the Video I Have Created Follow Key Codes and Conventions of Documentary Production?'

You can see from the way they are worded that they are less to do with the process of making the videos, and more about links with theory. The student in the first example has clearly read up on film theory and the essay question alone indicates this: to discuss the 'concept of the monstrous female' you can see that the student is doing a psychoanalytical reading of horror films. The student has also used the term 'representation'.

The student who wrote the second question has done some reading on key codes and conventions in documentary and therefore is able to analyse their own work using these as a framework. The content of the essay will discuss what the student did, but it is not a description, it is an analysis of the student's own work after doing some reading on how documentaries are constructed.

Advice on Writing Critical Reflection and Analysis Essays

Academic reading is essential for this type of essay because it will demonstrate that you know a lot about the topic that you are discussing, and this will give your essay substance. Doing some substantial reading and research in the early stages of your project, creating a list of quotes that will influence your work, and which will subsequently be used in the essay is a good place to start.

Keywords you could use in researching for wider reading could include:

- representation and stereotyping;
- realism;
- ideology;
- preferred reading;
- narrative;
- genre;
- encoding and decoding;
- gender;
- ethnicity;
- mise en scène.

The **introduction** of your essay should give a brief overview of what it is going to be about. This is where you reveal your key arguments, readings and the examples that you are going to use. You can even use a quotation here that establishes the key ideas that you are going to discuss.

In the **main body** of the essay you will explore the key ideas in more depth, providing evidence from your reading, and then applying the key ideas and concepts to your own work. Referring to your own work here will illustrate your understanding of the key ideas.

The number of paragraphs that you include in the main body of the essay varies according to essay length, but paragraphs average at roughly 100 words each. Therefore, a 2000-word essay will have approximately 20 paragraphs.

Each paragraph should contain one key idea with a series of supporting sentences, perhaps with an appropriate quote. So, for example, in a paragraph you could introduce a key point, then include a quotation to support it. You could then follow this with an example from your own media text that you are analysing. For example:

> Horror films are strongly built around gender and more specifically built around a subconscious dread of differences between the sexes. Barry Keith Grant says that 'the horror film … is preoccupied with sexual difference and gender' (Grant, 1996: 1). Our fear of horror films comes from its deconstructing of genders that attack and disturb ideas about our own identity. This was the main aim of my own horror movie, to convey men's fear of women through castration and the portrayal of women as a monstrous figure within horror movies.

In breaking down the paragraph above into its key components, we can see that it has the following structure:

- The student introduces the main point in the opening sentence: 'a subconscious dread of differences between the sexes'.

- This idea is then supported by a quote: '"the horror film … is preoccupied with sexual difference and gender"' (Grant, 1996: 1).

- The student then elaborates on this to demonstrate that they have understood the reading: 'Our fear of horror films comes from its deconstructing of genders that attack and disturb ideas about our own identity.'

- Finally, the student links the theory to their own work: 'This was the main aim of my own horror movie …'

For the **conclusion** you should summarise your key argument, and no new ideas should be introduced at this stage. Conclusions should be kept brief and to the point, and you can refer back to the main points you raised in the introduction.

You could also split the whole essay into sections using subheadings. This will help to organise your essay into a clear argument, and will help the reader to identify the structure. Thinking of an essay in this way helps you to understand how many points to make and how to structure them clearly.

An essay of this sort could be enhanced by illustrations that provide evidence and examples of the points being made. You could use screenshots from the video and scans from the storyboard to illustrate points where appropriate.

You should provide references throughout your essay, using whatever referencing system is the accepted standard. Providing evidence of wider reading of academic texts for a brief of this nature is very important and will help enhance your work.

The **bibliography** should list all the reading you have done for the essay. It should only include texts that you have actually referenced in the essay. It should be presented in alphabetical order by author's name.

Critical Reflection and Analysis of the Process of the Media Project

Another area of focus for critical reflection and analysis is on the *process* of the media project. You will focus here on the way the project was realised and the contribution you made to it. The following exercise will help you to assess the effectiveness of your team, and your own contribution to it. Such reflection will also be valuable in enhancing your employability. For example, it could give you an insight into aspects of your own approach to teamwork and some evidence that you could point to in a job-interview situation. An annual appraisal in your career is also an example of when such reflective skills will be of value in the workplace.

EXERCISE
Assessment and Evaluation of Your Project Team

This exercise will help you to assess the effectiveness of your project team. Use the following assessment criteria to aid your evaluation:

- The effectiveness of the project team's organisation.
- The effectiveness of the team's time-management.
- The effectiveness of the team's problem-solving.
- How the team divided the labour.
- Evidence of the team's technical skills.
- Evidence of the team's communication.
- Evidence of the team's motivation and enthusiasm throughout the project.
- The effectiveness of the team's work with the project client.
- The level of professionalism demonstrated by the team.

For each of the above criteria, offer some examples and evidence to justify your evaluation/assessment. Follow this up by thinking of some strengths and weaknesses and some strategies for improving on the teamwork for the project if you were to repeat it in future.

EXERCISE
Analysis of Your Team Role in the Media Project

The following exercise will form the basis of a critical reflection report. We will discuss report writing later in the chapter, but first you should analyse what type of teamworker you are, pointing out some positive and negative features of your group work.

In Chapter 2 we discussed the different ways you might contribute to a project team by characterising some features of different levels of contribution to a media project. We presented six typical characteristics of individual team members of student projects. This is repeated below to help you to analyse and reflect on your own contribution to the group work you have been engaged with. Start by reading the team member types listed below and identifying which one you feel is most reflective of you.

The absentee: This person does not work effectively as part of a team. They are often absent and prefer to work on their own. They have poor communication skills, and lack commitment to a shared purpose. They will follow others' lead and contribute little of value or relevance to the project. Their organisational skills will be disruptive of the team.

The clock-watcher: This group member's attendance and engagement with the project subsides after a positive and proactive start. They offer a reasonable amount to the project, but tend to stick within their comfort zone throughout. They lack attention to detail and have a 'this'll do' attitude to their work.

The good teamworker: This person has good attendance and engagement with the project. They follow rather than lead others, and might shy away from the important decisions. Or they might have unrealistic aims for the project. They sometimes prioritise other commitments such as their leisure pursuits, work and other coursework deadlines. Their communication and organisational skills could be improved.

The overseer: This group member is very conscientious, and extremely hard working in all aspects of the project. However, this might be to their downfall. They may be seen as being quite bossy for taking too much control over the project. Their leadership is not effective, in that it may fragment the group. This person can be over-confident and unable to take advice from others. Or they can be overly critical of their own and others' work.

The very good teamworker: This group member is very co-operative within the group. They show initiative, they stop the team from prevaricating and are very good at completing tasks straight away. They can solve problems by being flexible, they have good creative vision and lots of ideas. They are very good at communicating and have well-developed networking skills.

The first-class teamworker: This team member has excellent leadership qualities. They thrive on challenges and enjoy taking responsibility. They set goals, are highly motivated. They hold the group together. They show lots of enthusiasm for the project, and encourage enthusiasm in others. They listen to and support everyone else's ideas. They have a keen awareness of quality control, and an excellent attention to detail. They work well with others to a shared purpose.

Now that you have identified which of the above team characteristics fits you best, think of some examples and evidence from your experience of media project work that supports the team characteristic you have identified with most closely. Select the criteria below that fit most closely to your own contribution to the teamwork for the project you are evaluating. Think of some examples and evidence to illustrate your own contribution to the project – both good and bad!

Tips for effective teamwork				
Try to think outside the box	Try to be innovative, original and creative	Try always to be assertive and positive	Be open to new ideas and new experiences	Try to be a problem solver
Take steps to maintain enthusiasm within the team	Prioritise honesty in everything you do	Try to be mature at all times	Try to be supportive of others within the team	Try to motivate your teammates
Think positively as a starting point within the project	Do all you can to help in the decision making	Strive for excellence at all times but be aware of times when you should back off	Be aware of your own skills and how to use them to the benefit of the team	Be organised and plan ahead and use time-management techniques to enable this
Pay attention to detail at all times	Be highly engaged with the project throughout	Try to lead the team when appropriate and develop your leadership skills	Try to complete tasks straight away through effective time management	Be open with your ideas and flexible in applying them

Tips for avoiding ineffective teamwork				
Avoid being over precious about your own contribution	Try to avoid being defensive about your involvement in the project	Try to avoid prioritising other commitments	Try to not fail to follow through any commitments you make	Try not to dominate proceedings within the teamwork
Don't take credit for too much of the project	Avoid over-delegating tasks	Try not to take too much on in the project	Avoid being over negative about aspects of the project	Try not to undermine your teammate's within the teamwork
Don't avoid conflict when an airing of feelings would help	Try to avoid being over critical of your own or other people's work for the project	Try to avoid being too resistant to change and new ideas within the project	Try to stop perfectionism taking hold of you	Avoid dismissing areas of the project you are not interested in or feel uncomfortable with
Try to avoid blaming others for team failings	Avoid a lack of attendance being a reason for the rest of the team to dismiss your contribution	Try to avoid the temptation to work on your own for the project which is really a group project	Avoid a 'this'll do' attitude to the work on the project	Try to avoid being too much of a follower of the team throughout the project

FIGURE 11.3
Tips for effective teamwork, and tips for avoiding ineffective teamwork

For example, you might say 'I consider myself to be a "very good teamworker" because I always tried to motivate my teammates. For example, I organised a lunch meeting where we ate together and planned work. This boosted the team morale. However, I do feel I could improve by trying not to take too much on and by delegating more effectively. On one occasion, as well as being the designated producer I was trying to advise the camera operator and actors on how to do their job. In future I will stick to my own role and have faith in others' abilities.'

Critical Reflection on the Process of a Media Project

The suggested essay questions given previously in this chapter have enabled a focus on the product of your media project, encouraging analysis of aspects of media and cultural theory. Another source of critical analysis is to reflect on the *process* of the project itself. Rather than simply describing what you did, this requires you to analyse and reflect critically on the experience. We will examine ways you can reflect on the process of the project in the form of a written report, but first we consider ways of approaching reflective writing.

Reflective Writing

According to Jenny Moon (2004), an expert in reflective writing and critical thinking, you can increase the level of depth in the process of your reflective writing by moving away from pure description towards deep reflection. An overly descriptive account is simple and basic, and lacks analysis. It is mostly presented from one point of view, asks no questions and offers no alternative scenarios. It does not develop an argument or position and is written as a simple sequence of events.

When writing a reflective report you should divide it into sections, each focusing on a key point, such as team dynamics, the process of research, constraints and determinants, and so on. You should then reflect on each key point, observing the following features of deep, reflective writing as highlighted by Moon:

- The key point being made in each section is observed from multiple perspectives.
- A recognition that events exist in specific contexts.
- The motives of other people are compared and contrasted with those of you, the writer.
- A self-questioning and an 'internal dialogue'.
- An ability to stand back from an event and analyse objectively.
- A recognition that prior experience can have an influence on your work.
- An understanding that learning from your experience can influence future action.

For each key point that you are making about your experience of the media project work you could follow this system in order to move from description to deep reflection:

- First, describe what happened.
- Second, describe the outcome of what happened.

EVALUATING YOUR MEDIA PROJECTS

- Third, discuss your response to what happened, and the reactions of others.
- Next, make connections with your learning from prior experience.
- Then, think about how you might have approached the situation differently.
- Next, say how this would have affected the outcome.
- Finally, explain what you have learned from this and how this will influence your future approach.

EXERCISE
Writing a Reflective Report

A report format is useful for this type of reflection, and is a form of writing that will contribute to your employability skills base too. The following structure can be used as a guideline.

- **Title page** – to include the title of the report, the author's name and the current date. This page can be illustrated and designed with graphics.
- **Contents page** – to include a list of the main sections and sub-sections with page numbers.
- **Summary page** – this gives a brief outline of the report including an introduction to the subject of the report and an explanation of the report's purpose. This should be no longer than a page in length.
- **Main body** – this should contain the main substance of the report detailing your findings under subheadings. It should be analytical, constructive and reflective as encouraged above. You should think about how you will organise this and the subject of each subheading.
- **Subheadings** – you could select some of the subheadings from the following list to focus your analysis of your own contribution to the project. For each, you will give evidence and examples to illustrate.
    - enthusiasm and commitment;
    - punctuality and attendance;
    - creative input;
    - practical input;
    - communication skills displayed;
    - professionalism displayed;
    - emotional intelligence displayed.
- **Conclusions page** – in this section you will draw together the main points of the report to give an overview of the findings.
- **Recommendations page** – and in this section you should follow on from the conclusions and identify a time frame for their achievement. Your recommendations should be *specific, measurable* and *achievable*. State the action to be taken in future by yourself as a result of the report's content. The recommendations should be numbered in a list.
- **Appendices** – this is supplementary information and evidence to assertions made in the report. This is not usually included in the word count, if one is set.

Summary

In this chapter we have considered how to assess and evaluate both the *product* and the *process* of your media project. You have been asked to consider your own work in the wider context of a media degree, making connections between practice and theory.

You have practised reflecting on the part that you played within your team, and have analysed team dynamics. You have gained an insight into essay and report writing that will enable you to reflect critically on your work, and working practices. Honing your critical reflection and analysis is a useful employability skill. In the following, and final, chapter we will consolidate the knowledge you have gained from this book, and examine this further within the context of your future employment.

Further Reading

Further information to support the exercise on the grammar of the shot and edit can be found in the following books:

Bowen, Christopher, and Thompson, Roy, 2009, *Grammar of the Shot*, Oxford: Focal Press.

Bowen, Christopher J., and Thompson, Roy, 2013, *Grammar of the Edit*, Oxford: Focal Press.

Recommended reading as a starting point for some of the essay titles listed in this chapter includes:

Affron, Charles, and Affron, Mirella Jona, 1995, *Sets in Motion*, New Brunswick, NJ: Rutgers University Press.

Bellantoni, Patti, 2012, *If It's Purple, Someone's Gonna Die: The Power of Color in Visual Storytelling*, Oxford: Focal Press.

Bordwell, David, and Thompson, Kristin, 2017, *Film Art*, New York: McGraw-Hill.

Curran Bernard, Sheila, 2016, *Documentary Storytelling*, Oxford: Focal Press.

Doane, Mary Anne, 1985, 'Ideology and the Practice of Sound Mixing' in Weis, Elizabeth, and Belton, John (eds), *Film Sound: Theory and Practice*, New York: Columbia University Press.

Gonzales Crisp, Denise, 2012, *Typography*, London: Thames & Hudson.

Orpen, Valerie, 2009, *Film Editing: The Art of the Expressive*, London: Wallflower.

Pramaggiore, M., and Wallis, T., 2008, *Film: A Critical Introduction*, London: Laurence King Publishing.

Raskin, Richard, 2002, *The Art of the Short Fiction Film: A Shot by Shot Study of Nine Modern Classics*, London: McFarland & Company.

Street, Sarah, 2001, *Costume and Cinema: Dress Codes in Popular Film*, London: Wallflower.

For more information on general essay writing and critical reflection skills, look at:

Godfrey, Jeanne, 2011, *Writing for University*, Basingstoke: Palgrave Macmillan.

Godfrey, Jeanne, 2013, *How to Use Reading in Your Essays*, Basingstoke: Palgrave Macmillan.

Marshall, Lorraine, and Rowland, Frances, 2006, *A Guide to Learning Independently*, Frenchs Forest, NSW: Pearson Longman (pp. 210–223).

Moon, J., 2004, *A Handbook of Reflective and Experiential Learning: Theory and Practice*, London: Routledge.

12

EMPLOYABILITY AND MEDIA PRACTICE
Becoming Career-Ready

After reading this chapter you will be able to:

- analyse the skills you have developed through practical media work that could be transferable to an employment context;
- produce essential employability material, such as a CV, a portfolio to help you become career-ready;
- practise finding jobs and answering practice interview questions.

Introduction

This final chapter returns to the beginning of the book and concerns itself with the link between media practice and employability. Chapter 1 considered how a range of important skills appropriate to the jobs market can be developed through engaging with media-practice work on your degree course. This chapter will help you to focus on what you could do to make yourself as career-ready as possible. It will summarise how to use the skills in critical analysis and reflection from the previous chapter, and your experience of project work, and consider how this can feed into potential future careers.

The exercises in this chapter will be useful for your career development as preparation for applying for work in the media and creative industries. This includes the creation of a career planning report in which you conduct research on a chosen career path, and draw together the knowledge gained from this book, and your degree course as a whole.

Analysing and Reflecting on Transferable Skills

In the previous chapter you were encouraged to reflect on practical media work you have been engaged with. Much of this reflection was carried out in the context of identifying skills developed through media projects that might be transferable to the workplace. The following exercise encourages you to audit the skills that will be valuable to future employers.

EXERCISE
Identifying Skills and Qualities
Required by Employers

The list in Figure 12.1 is based on criteria employers use to evaluate potential candidates for work in the media and creative industries. It has been collated from job descriptions and person specifications for a wide variety of creative industries jobs. At this stage, it will be useful for you to create a skills audit and evaluate your level of competence in these skills.

The first column lists the skills that employers require. In the second column, rate your level of competence. In the third column, give an example of where you have demonstrated this skill. This could be an example from your course, work experience, volunteering or extra-curricular activities and hobbies. In the final column, suggest a strategy for improving and developing each of the skills listed.

Personal Skills Audit			
Skill List	Level of Competence 1 = Poor 5 = Excellent	Example	Strategy for Development of Skill
Research ability and analytical skills			
Organisational skills, and an ability to multi-task			
Time-management skills			
Ability to work to deadlines and cope with periodic increases in workload			
Communication, negotiation and interpersonal skills			
Administrative skills			

Technical media skills (camerawork, editing, web development, and so on)			
Ability to work to a brief, project-management skills, and problem solving			
Social media and networking skills			
Written, spoken and presentation skills			
Ability to be innovative and creative			
Ability to show motivation, initiative, be proactive and adapt to change			
Ability to work successfully both within a team and on own initiative			
Ability to accept feedback			
Awareness of cultural and social diversity			
Leadership and management skills			
Ability to show enthusiasm and positivity and sustained commitment to a shared purpose			

FIGURE 12.1
Personal skills audit

Use the results of this exercise to develop a list of skills that you could offer to future employers when applying for work. We will return to this list when looking at CV production and job interviews later in this chapter.

Asking for References

When you graduate, you will always be asked for references when applying for jobs. There are two types of reference. An academic reference is usually provided by your university and simply states what you achieved in terms of grades. A character reference is more detailed and includes some of the skills you demonstrated through your degree, such as those in the skills audit we outlined previously.

Your potential employer will request two (or sometimes three) references for your job application. It is then your responsibility to ask for references from people who know you well enough to comment on your skills. The referees should have worked with you or known you relatively recently.

The first reference could come from your course leader or personal tutor. The second reference may come from a current employer or one of your work experience/placement providers. Your brief provider and client for your media project brief might be a potential referee too. You will need to pass on contact details to the employer so that they can request the references directly from the referees. An employer will usually only ask to see the references if they are considering offering you a job after interview.

It is important to ask your referees if they are happy to write a character reference for you, before passing on their contact details to the employer. Nobody takes kindly to reference requests from employers relating to students who have not asked referees about it beforehand!

Sometimes a tutor will ask you to write down some pointers about what you would like them to say. The following exercise will help you to do this.

EXERCISE
Drafting Your Own Reference

It is important that you understand how much detail a potential employer will be asking about you when they request a reference. It will help to give your referees details about yourself in order that the reference can be composed to suit you individually. Start by reminding them of who you are and the context in which your chosen referee knows you. Give them brief information about the job (or course) that you are applying for. Provide a copy of your CV, if appropriate. Also, a short resumé of what you would like your referee to mention including work experience, extra-curricular activities, your career aims, and strengths and weaknesses on your degree.

The following is a list of the sorts of questions that your referee will be asked to answer about you. They will always be asked 'How long have you known the candidate and in what capacity?' at the beginning of the reference, and at the end they will be asked whether they would recommend you for the job. Choose some of the questions in Figure 12.2 to add to the draft of your reference. Write some notes about your strengths and skills and what you have to offer. These notes can act as a rough guide to what you would like your referee to mention when they write a reference for you.

How long have you known the candidate and in what capacity?	How would you rate the candidate's written and spoken communication skills?	Can you comment on the candidate's practical and creative skills?
What are their organisational and time-management skills like?	Do they face challenges well, and are they able to work under pressure?	What is their academic ability and record on their degree?
What is their predicted or actual degree result?	How would you rate the candidate's participation in university life and extra-curricular engagement?	What was their level of commitment, and how hard did they work?

Can you comment on any work experience the candidate carried out during their time at university?	How would you rate personal factors such as motivation, maturity, honesty, reliability, and so on...?	Can you comment on the candidate's interpersonal and teamwork skills?
What was the candidate's record of attendance, time keeping, and punctuality like?	How would you rate the candidate's interest in, understanding of, and suitability for the employment area being applied for?	**Would you recommend the candidate to us?**

FIGURE 12.2
Questions for referees

CVs and Covering Letters

Whether you go on to work as a freelance or as an employee in the creative industries sector, you will benefit from having a curriculum vitae (CV). This, along with a covering letter (or email) and possibly also portfolio (see below), will be invaluable to you in your search for work. You may be asked to submit a CV and covering letter (or email) for a job application, or to attach your CV to a completed application form.

Your CV is a way of summarising the skills and attributes you can offer to potential employers. Your university careers (or employability) department will be able to help you with access to CV building software along with advice. There are also many useful resources available online to support production of your CV including downloadable templates, and useful guidance about what employers are looking for.

There are many types of CV appropriate to different types of jobs, but a standard CV should at least include the elements detailed in Figure 12.3, and be kept to no more than two sides of A4.

Your name
Address/es – term time/holiday time. Optional
Phone number/s – landline and mobile
Email address
Social media – such as LinkedIn/link to online portfolio/Twitter/Facebook/blog
Personal profile statement
Relevant work experience including voluntary work starting with the most recent. Include date, employer and further details including your role, skills developed and key responsibilities.
Key skills – a list with evidence and examples.

(Continued)

Education – date, name of institution, qualifications and grades with most recent first.	
References – give the names, brief contact details and position of two referees, or state 'references available on request'.	

FIGURE 12.3
Standard CV structure

Using the latest version of your CV (or that of a friend) use the checklist in Figure 12.4 to evaluate it and make appropriate changes.

Criteria for evaluation of CV	Evaluation			Comments and suggestions on improvements
Presentation of the CV				
Is it no more than 2 sides of A4 paper in length?	Yes	Partially	No	
If it were to be printed out and photocopied, would it be clear? Does it avoid colour and heavy shading?	Yes	Partially	No	
Is it clear and easy to scan?	Yes	Partially	No	
Does it make use of headings and subheadings?	Yes	Partially	No	
Does it use short paragraphs and bullet points to assist layout?	Yes	Partially	No	
Is the font appropriate in style, size and colour?	Yes	Partially	No	
Is the spelling and grammar accurate?	Yes	Partially	No	
Is it written in note form or long form and whichever is chosen is it used consistently?	Yes	Partially	No	
Is there consistent use of positive action verbs such as led, delegated, devised, achieved, arranged, attained?	Yes	Partially	No	

Personal Information			
Is the name of the person included (without nicknames)?	Yes	Partially	No
Does it include the address of the applicant? This is optional, but if it is included is it the full address plus postcode?	Yes	Partially	No
Does it include the phone number/s of the applicant?	Yes	Partially	No
Does it include an appropriate email address which includes the applicant's full name?	Yes	Partially	No
Does it include (optional) addresses of professional social media accounts?	Yes	Partially	No
Does it exclude mention of age, gender, marital status, a photo?	Yes	Partially	No
Personal Profile			
Is the profile short and to the point?	Yes	Partially	No
Is the profile written in the third person?	Yes	Partially	No
Does the personal profile mention what has been achieved so far?	Yes	Partially	No
Does the profile avoid clichés?	Yes	Partially	No
Does the profile give evidence of key skills?	Yes	Partially	No
Key Skills			
Does it list the applicant's key skills?	Yes	Partially	No
Does it list both hard and soft skills?	Yes	Partially	No
Are the skills listed appropriate to the job applied for?	Yes	Partially	No

(Continued)

Does it give evidence and examples of key skills?	**Yes**	**Partially**	**No**	
Are languages mentioned if appropriate to the job being applied for?	**Yes**	**Partially**	**No**	
Is driving and full clean licence mentioned if appropriate to the job being applied for?	**Yes**	**Partially**	**No**	
Are interests and hobbies mentioned if appropriate to the job being applied for?	**Yes**	**Partially**	**No**	
Work Experience				
Does it list work experience relevant to the job applied for?	**Yes**	**Partially**	**No**	
Does the list of work experience include a range of experience of work from volunteering to internships to involvement in societies to paid work?	**Yes**	**Partially**	**No**	
Is the list of work experience in date order with most recent first?	**Yes**	**Partially**	**No**	
Does the list of work experience include the dates and details of the employer including web address?	**Yes**	**Partially**	**No**	
Does the list of work experience detail the role and responsibilities, skills developed and key achievements?	**Yes**	**Partially**	**No**	
Education and Qualifications				
Is the list of education and qualifications listed in date order with the most recent first?	**Yes**	**Partially**	**No**	
Does the list of education include the dates attended and name of institution?	**Yes**	**Partially**	**No**	
Are the qualifications listed and is a grade given for the main ones, avoiding long lists of grades?	**Yes**	**Partially**	**No**	
Is there mention of the modules studied on the degree course where relevant to the job being applied for?	**Yes**	**Partially**	**No**	

References			
Does it include details of 2 referees giving their name, employer, job role and brief contact details?	**Yes**	**Partially**	**No**	
If it does not include referee details does it read 'References available upon request'?	**Yes**	**Partially**	**No**	
Are the referees appropriate, up to date, from the current course and work experience and appropriate to the job being applied for?	**Yes**	**Partially**	**No**	

FIGURE 12.4
CV checklist form

Composing a Cover Letter

Now that you have created a CV following the guidelines given above, you should also draft a cover letter. A covering letter (which may actually be in the form of an email) is an introduction that sets the context of your CV. It should be no more than half a page long. It should introduce yourself, specify what job you are applying for, why you are interested in the role, and what you believe you could bring to the company. Use this cover letter in your emails when you send your CV to potential employers as an attachment. As with the CV, you should adapt your covering letter to suit the company or employer that you are writing to.

Building a Career Portfolio

As well as having an up-to-date CV to hand, you might benefit from having a career portfolio available when job hunting. A portfolio is essentially an extended CV with detail and examples of what you have to offer. It is a way of creating an online personal brand for yourself. Many jobs and areas of employment in the creative industries will require you to provide a portfolio in order to apply for work whether you are freelance or an employee. There are a number of online sites that you can sign up to (often free) to build a portfolio from a given template. This is best produced electronically and presented as a link on your CV, covering letter, email and so on. The following guidelines will support you in producing your career portfolio.

Tips and Hints for Producing a Career Portfolio

- Choose a portfolio production software app that is simple to use and possible to update. It could simply be a web production or blogging app and does not need to be a specialist portfolio production app.

- If you have a URL make sure it is short and appropriate, preferably giving only your full name. You may have to pay for such an address but it should be worthwhile, and money well spent.

- Make sure the link works when pasted into your CV, covering letter and so on.

- Use a clear and simple design that reflects your personal 'brand'. Pay attention to page layout and the use of bold, italics and underlining. Make use of bulleted lists to enable speed reading of your portfolio. Avoid large blocks of dense text.

- Pay attention to typeface and use design and colours that are plain, simple and professional.

- Try to write in a succinct and concise way with an appropriately professional register. Ensure the consistent use of tense and, if you choose to write in note form, that is fine as long as it is used consistently.

- The portfolio should be easy and simple to navigate and this should be clear from the home page.

Structuring Your Portfolio Content

There are no hard and fast rules about what to include, but the following is a list of possible sections and sub-sections:

The home page: This might include an 'About' section with brief information about you and what you have to offer potential employers. This could be a version of the personal profile on your CV. You should include mention of your career aspirations here. This might also include a photo of you, which should be appropriate and professional. Avoid using photos of you that are too casual, such as a selfie from a night out and so on! Buying a professionally taken headshot for this purpose would be money well spent, or alternatively you could engage the services of a good photographer friend. You should include your full name here and also links to appropriate social media. It goes without saying that you should only include social media sites that support your personal brand and are suitably professional. If you have set up social media pages for professional rather than personal use, make sure they have sufficient appropriate content. We will discuss your social media sites later in this chapter.

Work experience: List all the work experience that is appropriate to the career area you aspire to. Include information about what you did, when, and the skills you used and gained. Include a bit of information about the placement provider, perhaps through a link to their web page or a copy of their logo. Include examples of work you did whilst on placement. You could link this to the section on examples of work (see below). You should include examples of any voluntary, unpaid work you do as well as hobbies (such as writing a blog) as work experience. At the end of the day, these things are experience of work which need recognition. Give a short summary before each example of work experience to describe what it is about. Make sure you have permission to include details of the organisation on your portfolio.

Skills on offer: This could be a separate sub-section that lists the main skills you have to offer. Give some examples and evidence of each skill area that could be a link to your work experience or the section on examples of work. Refer back to the skills audit exercise at the beginning of this chapter for content here.

Examples of work: Use your portfolio to show examples of your work. This could be via links to websites, videos, photos, blogs, and so on, or it could be work that you embed in the pages. Only include your best and most relevant work and limit it to around ten pieces. Prioritise quality and appropriateness over quantity. Make sure you explain clearly what each example of work is, what role you had in it and what skills it demonstrates. If you are including videos, consider only putting an extract up or indicate the length of each. If you are including a showreel (a montage of extracts of your work on video) give a clear explanation of it and use onscreen text to guide the viewer. Limit the length and indicate how long it is.

CV: This section should be embedded so that it can be read whilst viewing the portfolio, but also downloadable as a separate PDF file. Make sure that when it is downloaded, the file is named with your full name and the fact that it is your CV.

Testimonials: This should include short written statements or testimonials about you and your services from appropriate people. This could be people you have worked for during placements, for example. It could be a quote from a reference you have been given. Make sure you ask permission and include the name of the referee and their job role and title.

Contacts page: You should include a sub-section to enable people to contact you. Include a clear and simple email address. You could also include your social media links here again. This could be a form for sending you a direct email too. Avoid including personal email addresses, phone numbers and your home address.

Use the form in Figure 12.5 to develop a plan for your career portfolio.

Structure of portfolio	Contents of portfolio	Ideas/notes of what to include in your portfolio
Homepage/ About Page	<ul><li>Full name</li><li>Professional photo of yourself</li><li>About section with brief information on what you have to offer</li><li>Link to professional social media and website</li><li>Index of contents/navigation bar</li><li>Description of your motivations and interests</li><li>Description of your future career ambitions</li><li>Statement on your work ethic and professional mission statement</li></ul>	

(Continued)

Structure of portfolio	Contents of portfolio	Ideas/notes of what to include in your portfolio
CV	• Include a link to your CV • Downloadable as a PDF	
Key Skills	• Include key skills under subheadings • Give examples and evidence for each skill area	
Work Experience	• List work experience with information about your role and what you achieved from it • Include internships, paid work, voluntary work and membership of clubs and societies • Give information about the organisation worked with (link to their website)	
Examples of work	• Sample of the best work (about 10) • Include a variety if possible • Include web pages, links to video, copies of projects, blogs and scans of essays. If it is video, say how long it is. • Give examples that reflect your strengths and skills • Explain each example in relation to why it is relevant to your career area of focus. • Include appropriate acknowledgements and copyright/ confidentiality information and obtain permission if needed	
Testimonials	• Collection of references or letters of recommendation from work experience employers, etc. • Obtain permission to give names, organisation and job role for anyone you quote	

Structure of portfolio	Contents of portfolio	Ideas/notes of what to include in your portfolio
Contact Page	• Include your email address • Include social media links again • Include a form for people to send you a direct email from the portfolio	

FIGURE 12.5
Career portfolio planning form

Now use the form in Figure 12.6 to evaluate your own portfolio or that of a peer. Use this to work out ways of improving your portfolio.

QUESTION	YES	NO	PARTIALLY	Suggestions for improvements
HOME PAGE	YES	NO	PARTIALLY	
If there's a photo is it appropriate/professional?				
Is the full name included?				
Is there a sense of a career aspiration?				
Is the typeface and design clean and simple/appropriate?				
Is there a sense of personal branding?				
Are there links to social media?				
Are the social media links appropriate and professional?				
Is the profile succinct and concise?				
Is it clear what career area is aspired to?				
Is the profile consistent and well laid out?				
Is note form used and if so is it consistently used?				

(Continued)

QUESTION	YES	NO	PARTIALLY	Suggestions for improvements
HOME PAGE	**YES**	**NO**	**PARTIALLY**	
Is there a consistent use of tense?				
Does it make use of bulleted lists?				
Does it make use of bold, colour and italics to highlight important points?				
Are there any typos/spelling mistakes?				
Are there any grammatical errors?				
CV (CURRICULUM VITAE)	**YES**	**NO**	**PARTIALLY**	
Is there a CV link included?				
Is it downloadable as a printable PDF?				
Is the CV shown on screen as well as being downloadable?				
KEY SKILLS	**YES**	**NO**	**PARTIALLY**	
Are key skills listed under subheadings?				
Are there examples and evidence given for each skill area?				
Does it avoid clichés?				
Do the skills link to the career area aspired to?				
WORK EXPERIENCE	**YES**	**NO**	**PARTIALLY**	
Does it list only work experience relevant to the career aspired to?				
Is there evidence of what was done and skills developed?				
Does it include examples and visuals?				
Does it include voluntary/unpaid work and hobbies such as writing a blog as work experience?				
If there are links to different sites (for example a blog site or a company) do they work?				

QUESTION	YES	NO	PARTIALLY	Suggestions for improvements
WORK EXPERIENCE	**YES**	**NO**	**PARTIALLY**	
Is there a short summary before each example of work experience to describe what it is about and how it is relevant?				
EXAMPLES OF WORK	**YES**	**NO**	**PARTIALLY**	
Are examples of work shown in the portfolio (showreel, videos, photos, projects)?				
Is there a clear explanation of what work is being shown and why?				
If showing videos (for example a showreel), is there an explanation of what the project was and its running time?				
Is there a sufficient amount of work shown to give evidence of ability?				
TESTIMONIALS	**YES**	**NO**	**PARTIALLY**	
Is there a section for testimonials?				
Are the testimonials appropriate?				
Has permission been sought to publish the comments?				
Are the testimonials attributed?				
CONTACT PAGE	**YES**	**NO**	**PARTIALLY**	
Is there a form to enable direct emailing?				
Is there an appropriate email address?				
Are there links to social media included?				
Are social media links suitably professional?				

FIGURE 12.6
Career portfolio evaluation form

Getting to Grips with Social Media: Social Media Makeover

In Chapter 10 we discussed the ways that you can use social media to advertise or create interest in specific projects that you are working on. We are now going to focus on how you should use social media to advertise *yourself*, and create a professional online presence.

Using social media to connect with family and friends is probably second nature to you. However, it is also a very useful tool for presenting your skills, qualities and experience to potential employers. Many employers look at applicants' social media profiles in order to determine whether the candidate is a suitable employee for their company. This is why the way you present yourself online is so important.

EXERCISE
Perform a Social Media Makeover

Ask a friend to search for your name online to reveal and report back to you what potential employers might see about you. You might be surprised at what crops up, just by typing your name into a search engine! Next, give your friend access to your online social media profiles, video- and photo-sharing sites, and blogs. Ask them to analyse the content, and draw up a simple character profile based on this. Now list any material or information that might show you in a poor light. For example, casual photos of your social life, or bad language and unprofessional conduct. In light of the above, consider whether it might be a good idea to adjust your privacy settings. *Do all you can to separate the social from the professional!*

You are now in a strong position to develop a professional online profile, for example through LinkedIn if you don't already have an account. In this profile you could include links to your online portfolio and CV. A lot of the content may overlap, or repeat what is contained in your portfolio, but it is important that you have detail and depth in all avenues of your professional online profile.

Job Hunting

Be creative and logical in your search for jobs. Use LinkedIn and Twitter to find and forge online networks. Sign up to specialist careers sites in the area that you are interested in such as Creative Skillset and Creative Choices for opportunities in the creative industries. Try BBC Academy and Shooting People for roles in media production. This list is long and the deeper you dig the more openings you can make for yourself. Follow the social media sites of organisations you are interested in, and look at what other individuals and organisations are linked to these accounts. Be aware that the type of job you are looking for might not necessarily be advertised online – it is up to you to seek out available opportunities. You should also make use of your university's careers and employability department.

Interviews

So far you have worked hard to construct an outward-facing identity to share with potential employers. You've also learned how to create a CV and portfolio. However good your online profile appears, it is how you present yourself face-to-face that will determine whether you get the job or not. It is important that your personal presence matches your online profile.

There is a wealth of material available online about how to best approach interview situations, and you are advised to look at this. What we are interested in here, however, are the types of questions you may be asked in an interview or networking situation, and how best to answer them. The following exercise is an interview simulation that gives you an opportunity to practise answering some of the typical sorts of questions employers ask.

EXERCISE
Interview Simulation Questions

First, find a job advert and application details (including the job description and person specification) for a job you would be interested in applying for. Next, choose one question from each of the eight sections below. These questions follow a standard structure for interviews with opening and closing questions, and questions in between about yourself, your skills and your experience.

When answering each question, you should identify an example or evidence to illustrate your points. For this you could use the STARR mnemonic as follows. This will help you to structure your answer, and to add focus, depth and appropriate detail:

- S = SITUATION – describe the situation.
- T = TASK – describe what was expected of you.
- A = ACTION – describe what you did.
- R = RESULT – describe the outcome.
- R = REFLECTION – describe an alternative approach to the same situation.

Answer each of the questions you have chosen using the STARR mnemonic as a guide in the interview planning form in Figure 12.7.

QUESTION					
Opening questions					
What attracts you to our organisation?					
What did you do to prepare for this interview?					

(Continued)

QUESTION					
Questions about you					
How would your friends and fellow students describe you?					
What achievement do you feel most proud of?					
Questions about the organisation					
What have you found out about this organisation in your research?					
What do you think you can bring to the job you are applying for?					
Questions about the job					
What experience can you bring to the job you are applying for?					
What would you like to achieve within the first 6 months?					
Questions about your work experience					
Give an example of when you worked effectively in a team during work experience.					
Give an example of your effective problem solving whilst on work experience.					
Questions about your skills					
Give an example of when you did not succeed at something.					
What is your best developed skill?					
Questions about your ambition					
Where do you see yourself in 5 years' time?					

QUESTION					
What is your ultimate career aspiration?					
End questions					
How do you think your references might read?					
What questions would you like to ask about the job?					

FIGURE 12.7
Interview simulation planning form

You could follow this up by role playing an interview scenario with a friend or by arranging a mock interview with your university's employability department.

Career-Planning Report

Using what you have developed so far in this chapter, you can begin to develop a career plan. A written career plan is a very useful tool to help guide you upon graduation, so it is worth spending some time focusing on this to refer to later. This could make a fascinating read for yourself ten years down the road, to see if your career aspirations went to plan! Use this report to consolidate your research into your chosen career path and then use it as a guide to your aspirations. Keep it updated and return to it each time you apply for a job.

EXERCISE
Write a Career-Planning Report

Use the guidelines below to structure your report and to inform its content.

Title page: This should include the title of the report, for example 'My career plan', your name and the date. This page should be designed and laid out in an appropriate way, perhaps echoing the design of your online portfolio.

Contents page: List the main sections of the report, and use sub-sections if necessary, with page numbers. Include a list of illustrations and appendices.

Summary page: This is a brief outline of the report including an introduction to the subject of the report and the report's purpose; for example, 'A report on my career planning to date with a view to future employment in PR and marketing'.

Introduction page: The introduction includes more detail than the summary. You should identify the background to the report. You should also identify the objective, purpose and use of the report.

Main body: This is the substance of the report detailing the main points under subheadings. It should be analytical, constructive and reflective, and will include several sub-sections. For example, you might write about the following topics, all in relation to your future career plan:

- your career aspirations including case studies of people in the role you aspire to;
- research into your chosen career, including examples of job descriptions and adverts, and where they can be found;
- reflecting on your work experience, including details about tasks performed and problems solved;
- analysing your key skills, including what you have to offer, with examples and evidence;
- analysing the relevance of your degree and other educational experience to your future career;
- a timeline of your goals and career objectives, and a plan of action;
- evaluating the work you have done so far in enhancing your employability, including your career materials such as your CV, portfolio, social media profiles, experience of interviews and so on.

Conclusions page: Summarise the main points that you have made so far; do not introduce any new ideas or topics here.

Recommendations page: This follows on from the conclusions page. List actions to be taken in future by yourself as a result of the content of the report. For example, if you plan to broaden your networking experiences, you could include this here. Similarly, you could recommend to yourself that you seek further work experience that is relevant to your chosen path.

These should appear in a bulleted list, and *each* recommendation should be SMART as follows:

- **Specific** – Make sure it is clear and focused.
- **Measurable** – Make sure you can measure its success.
- **Advantages** – Identify how it will benefit you in future.
- **Realistic** – Make sure it is achievable.
- **Timescale** – Create a timetable for achieving it.

Appendices: This is a section where you should include any supplementary information and material that is not necessary in the main body of the report, but may have been referred to. Only include material that adds extra detail on what you have mentioned in the main body of the report. Appendices are not included in the word count of the report. Each should be numbered and have a title that describes its content.

You can have as many appendices as you wish, but all should be referred to in the main body. For example, you might have an appendix to show your career timeline, or screenshots from your career portfolio, or a copy of your CV. You could include a copy of a reference received and details of a live job advert as an example of the sort of job that would be your ideal.

Summary

Writing a career-planning report is a good point to end on, both in this chapter, and for the book as a whole. All the skills, knowledge and practical experience you have gained here have aimed to help you to become career-ready. By following the exercises and recommendations in this book you should now be able to identify your personal strengths and apply them to your chosen career plan and aspirations. This will enable you to access graduate-level employment with the confidence required for success.

Good luck!

GLOSSARY OF TERMS

The following words and terms listed in the glossary are defined here in the context of this book, and in the context of your media-practice projects.

Accelerated montage   A method of cross-cutting between two subjects; for example, during a chase sequence. Each subsequent shot of the two subjects decreases in length so that the pace of the sequence quickens to imply speed.

Anchorage   The application of words to an image in order to define or 'anchor' the image's meaning.

Appendix   The section in a report where you include supplementary information and material that is not necessary in the main body of the report.

Artificial light   Any lighting other than daylight that is created artificially for a scene – for example, electric light from a domestic lampshade, studio lighting, candle light, and so on. See also natural light.

Audience demographics   The classification of audiences by age, gender, race, level of education, and so on.

Blogging   The production of a written website with informal and informational posts similar to a diary entry. See also vlogging.

Camera movement   The use of motivated camera movement such as pan, tilt, cant, track and zoom to enhance communication.

Cant   A motivated camera movement that moves diagonally across the frame.

Career portfolio   A portfolio of evidence of your skills and experience used for job applications. It may be hard copy or more usually produced as a website.

Cinematography   The art of camera work and the use of light for film-making.

Classical continuity editing   This refers to a system of editing that developed in Hollywood during the classical era (approximately 1920–1960). Continuity is observed across different shots in a sequence, so that subject position and movement within the frame appear continuous. It is an ideological process that is largely taken for granted by audiences.

Classical Hollywood   The period of Hollywood between approximately 1920 and 1960 in which the studio system of production existed.

Client-led   A project in which a client provides the brief for your work.

Colour theory   A consideration of the emotional and cultural effects of colour, and how audiences respond to it.

Commutation test   A test in which different elements of mise en scène in an image (characters, settings, props, costume) are altered to change important parts of the meaning.

Composition   Techniques used in film-making that involve the arrangement of visual elements to form harmony and to enhance communication.

Content elements   Elements of the mise en scène such as character, costume, setting and props that provide a media text with 'content' and enable the audience's understanding of that text. See also technical elements.

Covering letter   A letter (or email) that accompanies a copy of your CV in a job application. It outlines what you are applying for and the main reasons for your application.

Copyright   Copyright refers to the ownership of a media text. This ownership usually belongs to the originator of the work, but can sometimes belong to a company or organisation.

Creative industries   The creative industries are a wide range of sectors including jobs for writers, musicians, computer programmers, public relations officers and retailers.

Critical analysis   Analysing the product of your media-practice project. This can include contextualising your work with media and cultural theory.

Critical reflection   Reflecting critically and objectively on the process of your media-practice project.

Curriculum vitae (CV)   A document used to show potential employers details about you including your skills, experience and qualifications.

Cut   A move from one shot to the next using continuity editing to help communicate meaning.

Cutaway   A technique used in editing. The layering of information to illustrate action or a point in more detail.

Diegetic and non-diegetic sound   Diegetic sound refers to any sound that appears from within the 'story' space of an audio-visual text (for example, dialogue and sound effects). Non-diegetic is its opposite; for example, a music track that is overdubbed in post-production to enhance mood.

Editing   The process of selecting and arranging footage to make a whole video or audio piece.

Elevator pitch   A short pitch, usually lasting for between 30 and 90 seconds. This is a useful way of presenting ideas or 'selling' a service in a concise and dynamic way.

Emotional intelligence   Having the ability to see how others might see you, and acting accordingly in professional situations.

Employability   The skillset required for the world of work.

Encoding and decoding   Encoding refers to the intended meaning that the producer of a text embeds within it. Decoding refers to the way in which the audience then 'reads' or understands the message.

Ethnographic research   A type of audience research that considers how demographics such as age, gender and nationality contribute to the ways audience members respond to media texts.

Fade   In editing, this is a gradual transition from black (fade-in) or to black (fade-out).

Fly-on-the-wall   A documentary format in which the camera crew follows the subject around observing and recording what happens.

Focus group   In audience research, this is a useful way of recording information and opinions through the form of a group discussion. The discussion can involve audio-visual recording and/or note-taking. The results are subsequently analysed using discourse analysis.

Framing   The selection of elements to include within the camera shot, or exclude from the shot.

Genre   This is a film studies term taken from the French word for types or kinds. It is a useful way of categorising media texts into recognisable and easily identifiable forms.

Hard skills and soft skills   Hard skills are practical and technical skills such as proficiency in using software, whereas soft skills refer to employability skills such as motivation, communication and showing initiative. See also transferable skills.

Ideology   In media and cultural studies this term refers to the construction of beliefs, which often occurs unconsciously, and is taken for granted by and accepted by audiences.

Jump cut   A hard edit that is created when portions are removed from a long take without a change in camera angle. This form of editing deliberately challenges the rules of classical continuity editing.

Kuleshov effect   This is an effect in montage editing in which two images which originally had no relation to each other are juxtaposed in order to construct a new meaning or 'third effect'. For example, the image of a person's face followed by the image of food constructs the meaning of hunger. See also montage and third effect.

Logline   A short description (usually one sentence) that distils a script down to its essential elements. Although brief, it should still be able to communicate a story. See also synopsis.

Looking room   Framing of a shot so that your subject looks 'into' the frame not out of the edge of the frame. This is also known as 'nose room'. The framing of people and characters in this way helps to create stability in an image. See also walking room.

Media literacy   Being literate and adept at using and expressing audio-visual language.

Methodology   The research methods you will use to analyse your work. For example, an analytical approach using cultural studies methodology such as representation, identity, gender, race, and so on.

Mise en scène   This is a film studies term that literally translates from French as 'putting into the scene'. It refers to the combination of settings, props, costumes, the position of characters within the frame, and how they interact with each other and the other elements in the picture.

Montage   Sometimes referred to as 'Soviet montage', this is a form of editing in which images are combined and contrasted in order to create an impression such as a political statement. See also Kuleshov effect and third effect.

Narrative   This is a way of organising our understanding of space and time into a cause-and-effect chain of events – the beginning, middle and end of a film or video, for example. Narrative encompasses the plot (the order in which events are represented), the story (the reconstruction of the events in a chronological order) and the narration (the way the plot is arranged).

Natural light   This refers to sunlight. It is the opposite of any type of light that has been artificially created or added to a scene. See also artificial light.

Networking   Meeting and interacting with likeminded people, potential employers, or clients. Networking can stretch your experience, and broaden your horizons.

Pan shot   A type of moving shot that moves horizontally from left to right or right to left on the tripod.

People skills   A set of interpersonal skills which demonstrate one's ability to work with people.

Personal development portfolio (PDP)   A portfolio of work that acts as a record of your knowledge and skills. You might keep this throughout your education to inform the production of a career portfolio or similar career tool.

Post-production   This term usually refers to editing. However, it can refer to a number of techniques that are applied to a media text after it is recorded or photographed; for example, digital editing, the addition of visual effects, photographic airbrushing and sound design.

Preferred reading   This is the preferred way that the producer of a media text intends their audience to 'read' and accept the text's message.

Press kit   A set of promotional materials to be used for marketing a product or organisation.

Press release   A written document about something noteworthy or newsworthy issued to the media for attracting wider publicity.

Process   The part of a project that is focused on whilst critically reflecting on it. This refers to the steps taken within the project from beginning to end.

Product   In the context of media project work, this refers to the media text that has been produced as a result of the project or process.

Proxemics   Derived from the word 'proximity', this is the arrangement and relationship between subjects (people) within the frame of a media text.

Quantitative and qualitative research   Quantitative research is a method of audience research that measures statistics such as 'how many', 'how often', and so on. It is usually conducted through the use of surveys and questionnaires. Qualitative research allows the audience to have a voice. It has more depth and concerns itself with how audiences use texts, and what texts mean to them. It considers them as individuals rather than an undifferentiated 'mass'.

Realism   Not to be confused with 'realistic'. Realism refers to the construction of the believability of events and characters within the confines of the text. For example, in classical Hollywood cinema, the narrative process (character, time, place) and continuity editing all contribute to the impression of 'realism'.

Recce   Short for 'reconnaissance' – this refers to checking out a location and assessing its suitability for your media projects.

Referee   The title given to somebody you ask to write a reference for you for job applications.

Release form   This is an agreement that is signed by a participant, or their parent or guardian, prior to being recorded, filmed or photographed. It is written proof that they have agreed to appear in your production. (Also called a consent form.)

Representation   This term is used to refer to the way people are characterised in media texts. It can refer to fictional and non-fictional representations and is often part of an ideological process.

Risk assessment   Workplace environments (such as filming locations) have to be assessed for their level of risk before work can be carried out there. This procedure involves filling in a risk assessment form to demonstrate that project participants are aware of potential hazards that might occur in the workplace.

Scenic breakdown   This is the breakdown of a story or script into a series of scenes, and brief description of the scenes' contents. It is a useful tool to produce prior to developing a storyboard.

Screenshot   The process of creating a still from a video or document to include in another document.

Self-awareness   Used in discussions of emotional intelligence to gauge a person's knowledge of themselves and how others perceive them.

Self and peer evaluation   The method of evaluating your own and your peers' contribution to a group project.

Semantic differential   This is a scale that measures a person or character's personality traits from very little to very much.

Showreel   A montage of extracts of your audio-visual work to show prospective employers.

Skills audit   A document that sets out a list of your key skills and rates your competence at each skill listed.

SMART objectives   A technique for ensuring that your objectives are based on criteria that make your goals meaningful.

STAR(R) mnemonic   A technique used in job interviews to ensure that answers to questions are detailed and reflective.

Stereotype   In media studies, this refers to the negative representation of people, usually a 'subordinate' group, in an oversimplified way.

Storyboard   A visual representation of a story or script in picture form. The images on the storyboard correspond with the shots that are planned for the finished audio-visual text.

Synopsis   This is a short, pithy summary of a narrative. See also logline.

Talking head   A documentary format that relies mostly on 'talking head' interviews as the main part of its content.

Team charter   A form completed by the team at the beginning of a project that outlines its scope and details. This ensures everyone has shared expectations of the project they are involved in.

Team code of conduct   An agreed list of behaviours for the production team to sign up to and to observe throughout the project.

Technical elements   The way that the content elements of a media text are manipulated using light, colour and visual effects. See also content elements.

Third effect   This refers to the effect in which meaning is constructed in post-production when images are juxtaposed with each other. For example, a close-up of a person's face followed by a shot of food produces a 'third effect' that implies hunger. See also Kuleshov effect and montage.

Three-act structure   A simple form of narrative structure that sets out the beginning, middle and end.

Tilt shot A vertical camera move, either upward or downward.

Tracking shot   A shot in which the camera follows the moving subject, usually with the aid of tracks (hence the name) or a camera 'dolly'.

Transferable skills   The employability skills that you can apply from one context to another; for example, from a media project to a professional workplace.

Typography   This refers to the style and arrangement of text; for example, on a web page, on an advertisement or in a video title sequence.

Uses and gratifications   This is a type of audience research that involves real participants in its study. It aims to find out how audience members use, and gain pleasure from using media.

Vanishing point   In composition, this is the point in which lines of perspective converge and disappear on the horizon line.

Vlogging   Conflation of video and blogging. Creating a video channel or site with informal and informational video posts. See also blogging.

Walking room   Framing of a shot so that the subject walks 'into' the space within the frame. The framing of people and characters in this way helps to create stability in an image. See also looking room.

Wild sound   Sometimes referred to as 'ambient sound'. This is sound recorded whilst filming (such as bird song or traffic noise) used to create a sense of aural space and as background noise.

Working title   Giving a name to your project, which may change before the project is completed.

BIBLIOGRAPHY

Affron, Charles, and Affron, Mirella Jona, 1995, *Sets in Motion*, New Brunswick, NJ: Rutgers University Press.

Alessandra, Pilar, 2010, *The Coffee Break Screenwriter*, Studio City, CA: Michael Wiese Productions.

Ashton, Paul, 2011, *The Calling Card Script: A Writer's Toolbox for Stage, Screen and Radio*, London: A & C Black.

Barker, Chris, 2000, *Cultural Studies: Theory and Practice*, London: Sage.

Barnwell, Jane, 2004, *Production Design: Architects of the Screen*, London: Wallflower.

Beek, Marco van, 2000, *A Practical Guide to Health and Safety in the Entertainment Industry*, Cambridge: Entertainment Technology Press.

Begleiter, Marcie, 2010, *From Word to Image: Storyboarding and the Filmmaking Process*, Studio City, CA: Michael Wiese.

Beiman, Nancy, 2007, *Prepare to Board! Creating Story and Characters for Animated Features and Shorts*, Oxford: Focal Press.

Bellantoni, Patti, 2012, *If It's Purple, Someone's Gonna Die: The Power of Color in Visual Storytelling*, Oxford: Focal Press.

Berger, John, 1977, *Ways of Seeing*, London: Penguin.

Birtwhistle, Andy, 2010, *Cinesonica: Sounding Film and Audio*, Manchester: Manchester University Press.

Bordwell, David, and Thompson, Kristin, 2017, *Film Art*, New York: McGraw-Hill.

Bowdin, Glenn, Allen, Johnny, O'Toole, William, Harris, Robert, and McDonnell, Ian, 2006, *Events Management*, London: Elsevier.

Bourdieu, Pierre, 2006, *Distinction: A Social Critique of the Judgement of Taste*, London: Routledge.

Bowen, Christopher J., and Thompson, Roy, 2009, *Grammar of the Shot*, Oxford: Focal Press.

Bowen, Christopher J., and Thompson, Roy, 2013, *Grammar of the Edit*, Oxford: Focal Press.

Bruzzi, Stella, 2006, *New Documentary*, London: Routledge.

Chandler, Daniel, 2007, *Semiotics: the Basics*, London: Routledge.

Cohen, Steve, and Shires, Linda, 1997, *Telling Stories, a Theoretical Analysis of Narrative Fiction*, London: Routledge.

Confederation for British Industry, 2009, *Future Fit: Preparing Graduates for the World of Work*, London: CBI.

Confederation of British Industry and National Union of Students, 2011, *Working Towards Your Future: Making the Most of Your Time in HE*, London: CBI.

Cottrell, Stella, 2008, *The Study Skills Handbook*, London: Palgrave Macmillan.

Curran Bernard, Sheila, 2016, *Documentary Storytelling*, Oxford: Focal Press.

Davies, Rosamund and Sigthorsson, Gauti, 2013, *Introducing the Creative Industries from Theory to Practice*, London: Sage.

Doane, Mary Anne, 1985, 'Ideology and the Practice of Sound Mixing' in Weis, Elizabeth, and Belton, John (eds), *Film Sound: Theory and Practice*, New York: Columbia University Press.

Fairweather, Rod, 1998, *Basic Studio Directing*, Oxford: Focal Press.

Frayling, Christopher, 2005, *Ken Adam, and the Art of Production Design*, London: Faber and Faber.

Gates, Richard, 2000, *Production Management for Film and Video*, Oxford: Focal Press.

Godfrey, Jeanne, 2011, *Writing for University*, Basingstoke: Palgrave Macmillan.

Godfrey, Jeanne, 2013, *How to Use Reading in Your Essays*, Basingstoke: Palgrave Macmillan.

Goleman, Daniel, 2004, *Emotional Intelligence and Working with Emotional Intelligence*, London: Bloomsbury.

Gonzales Crisp, Denise, 2012, *Typography*, London: Thames & Hudson.

Grant, Barry Keith, 1996, *The Dread of Difference: Gender and the Horror Film*, Texas: University of Texas.

Grove, Elliot, 2006, *Raindance Producers' Lab: Lo-to-no Budget Filmmaking*, Oxford: Focal Press.

Hall, Stuart, 1999, 'Encoding and Decoding' in During, Simon (ed.), *The Cultural Studies Reader*, London: Routledge.

Hall, Stuart, Evans, Jessica, and Nixon, Sean, 2013, *Representation*, London: Sage.

Halligan, Fionnuala, 2012, *Production Design*, Lewes: Ilex.

Harding, Thomas, 2001, *The Video Activists Handbook*, London: Pluto Press.

Harkins, Michael, 2013, *Understanding Type*, London: AVA Academia.

Hillner, Matthias, 2009, *Virtual Typography*, Lausanne; Worthing: AVA Academia.

Hinchliffe, G., and Jolly, A., 2010, *Employability and Graduate Identity: Investigating Graduate Identity*, Graduate Market Trends, University of East Anglia.

Hogan, Michael, 2014, 'The Secret Life of Students, review: an opportunity to despair', *The Telegraph*, 3 July (accessed online 27/09/2017).

Knapp, Mark, and Daly, John, 2011, *The SAGE Handbook of Interpersonal Communication*, London: Sage.

Kochberg, Searle (ed.), 2007, *Introduction to Documentary Production: A Guide for Media Students*, London: Wallflower.

La Motte, Richard, 2010, *Costume Design 101: The Business and Art of Creating Costumes for Film and Television*, Studio City, CA: Michael Wiese Productions.

Lambert, Beth, 2014, 'The Secret Life of Students: a Channel 4 documentary or an episode of Jeremy Kyle?', *New Statesman*, 4 July (accessed online 27/09/2017).

Landis, Deborah Nadoolman, 2012, *Costume Design*, Oxford: Focal Press.

Lyver, Des, and Swainson, Graham, 2005, *Basics of Video Lighting*, Oxford: Focal Press.

Maier, Robert G., 1994, *Location Scouting and Management Handbook*, London: Focal Press.

Marshall, Lorraine, and Rowland, Frances, 2006, *A Guide to Learning Independently*, Frenchs Forest, NSW: Pearson Longman.

McQuail, Denis, 2010, *McQuail's Mass Communication Theory*, 6th edition, London: Sage.

McQuail, Denis, Blumler, Jay G. and Brown, J. R., 1999, 'The Television Audience: A Revised Perspective' in Marris, Paul, and Thornham, Sue (eds), *Media Studies: A Reader*, Edinburgh: Edinburgh University Press.

Millerson, Gerald, 2006, *Lighting for Video*, Oxford: Focal Press.

Monaco, James, 2000, *How to Read a Film*, Oxford: Oxford University Press.

Moon, J., 2004, *A Handbook of Reflective and Experiential Learning: Theory and Practice*, London: Routledge.

Murch, Walter, 2001, *In the Blink of an Eye: A Perspective on Film Editing*, Los Angeles: Silman-James Press.

Musberger, Robert B., 2007, *An Introduction to Writing for Electronic Media: Scriptwriting Essentials Across the Genres*, Oxford: Focal Press.

Orpen, Valerie, 2009, *Film Editing: The Art of the Expressive*, London: Wallflower.

Parks, Stacey, 2007, *The Insider's Guide to Independent Film Distribution*, Oxford: Focal Press.

Pascale, Celine-Marie, 2013, *Social Inequality and the Politics of Representation*, London: Sage.

Petrie, Dennis, and Boggs, Joseph, 2012, *The Art of Watching Films*, New York: McGraw-Hill.

Pramaggiore, Maria, and Wallis, Tom, 2011, *Film: A Critical Introduction*, 3rd edition, London: Laurence King.

Rabiger, Michael, 2003, *Directing: Film Techniques and Aesthetics*, Oxford: Focal Press.

Raskin, Richard, 2002, *The Art of the Short Fiction Film: A Shot by Shot Study of Nine Modern Classics*, London: McFarland & Company.

Rowlands, Avril, 2000, *The Continuity Supervisor*, Oxford: Focal Press.

Saltz, Ina, 2011, *Typography Essentials*, Rockport: Gloucester, MA.

Shand, Ryan, and Craven, Ian, 2013, *Small-Gauge Storytelling: Discovering the Amateur Fiction Film*, Edinburgh: Edinburgh University Press.

Simon, Mark, 2000, *Storyboards: Motion in Art*, Oxford: Focal Press.

Starkey, Guy, 2000, 'Taking on the Tabloids: A Rationale for the Teaching of Media Practice', paper given at the AMPE conference, Bournemouth, September.

Street, Sarah, 2001, *Costume and Cinema, Dress Codes in Popular Film*, London: Wallflower.

Wayne, Mike, 1997, *Theorising Video Practice*, London: Lawrence & Wishart.

Wells, Paul, 2007, *Scriptwriting*, Singapore: AVA Publishing.

INDEX